Introvert

How to Thrive in an Extroverted World

(A Survival Guide on Managing Stress and Emotional Anxiety for Quiet People)

Darin Wood

Published By **Simon Dough**

Darin Wood

All Rights Reserved

Introvert: How to Thrive in an Extroverted World
(A Survival Guide on Managing Stress and
Emotional Anxiety for Quiet People)

ISBN 978-1-7780570-4-5

No part of this guidebook shall be reproduced in any form without permission in writing from the publisher except in the case of brief quotations embodied in critical articles or reviews.

Legal & Disclaimer

The information contained in this book is not designed to replace or take the place of any form of medicine or professional medical advice. The information in this book has been provided for educational & entertainment purposes only.

The information contained in this book has been compiled from sources deemed reliable, and it is accurate to the best of the Author's knowledge; however, the Author cannot guarantee its accuracy and validity and cannot be held liable for any errors or omissions. Changes are periodically made to this book. You must consult your doctor or get professional medical advice before using any of the suggested remedies, techniques, or information in this book.

Upon using the information contained in this book, you agree to hold harmless the Author from and against any damages, costs, and expenses, including any legal fees potentially resulting from the application of any of the information provided by this guide. This disclaimer applies to any damages or injury caused by the use and application, whether directly or indirectly, of any advice or information presented, whether for breach of contract, tort, negligence, personal injury, criminal intent, or under any other cause of action.

You agree to accept all risks of using the information presented inside this book. You need to consult a professional medical practitioner in order to ensure you are both able and healthy enough to participate in this program.

Table Of Contents

Chapter 1: The Unbearable Awkwardness Of Being An Introvert 1

Chapter 2: The Art Of Social Distancing .. 18

Chapter 3: The Joys Of Alone Time 26

Chapter 4: The Joys Of Eating Alone 43

Chapter 5: Why Introverts Need A Break Day Even From Their Specific Someone . 55

Chapter 6: How To Survive Parties 65

Chapter 7: The Art Of Small Talk For Introverts 72

Chapter 8: Finding Your Tribe 86

Chapter 9: The Introvert As A Romance Partner 94

Chapter 10: The Creative Introvert 109

Chapter 11: The Introvert's Guide To Networking 120

Chapter 12: The Benefits Of Being An Introvert 126

Chapter 13: The Introvert's Guide To Self-Care 132

Chapter 14: The Introvert's Path To Success 140

Chapter 15: Overcoming Introvert Stereotypes... 145

Chapter 16: The Future Of Introversion 151

Chapter 17: Understanding Your Introvert Nature... 157

Chapter 18: The Power Of Introverts ... 162

Chapter 19: Making Friends As An Introvert 169

Chapter 20: Surviving A World That Never Stops Talking.. 176

Chapter 1: The Unbearable Awkwardness Of Being An Introvert

Being an introvert can be a difficult revel in, specifically in a worldwide that appears to price extroversion and social competencies. Many introverts struggle with emotions of awkwardness and ache in social conditions, and can find it tough to connect with others or revel in like they belong. This financial disaster explores a number of the not unusual traumatic conditions that introverts face and offers techniques for coping and thriving in a international which can sense overwhelming.

But as they say, introverts are a super breed. Being an introvert is like being a hermit crab compelled to attend a beach birthday celebration. You try to aggregate in with the group, however deep down you without a doubt need to retreat into your shell and binge-watch your favourite TV display. While extroverts are busy making new pals and networking at events, introverts are stuck in the nook, pretending to text on their mobile cellphone honestly to avoid small communicate. But mind you, introverts are not miserable at the equal time as by myself. For maximum, it's miles their element. So if you're searching for to make plans with an introvert can be like playing a recreation of chess - you want to assume numerous actions earlier and anticipate their need for by myself time.

But the real kicker is while humans mistake introversion for rudeness. Just due to the reality I do now not need to interact in idle chitchat would now not mean I do no longer consisting of you. I'm no longer a hermit (or at least I suppose so); I sincerely want my by myself time to recharge. So, if you see me avoiding eye touch or sneaking out of a room, do no longer take it for my part. I'm surely seeking out to continue to exist in this extroverted international.

So we begin by using explaining what it method to be an introvert, and dispelling some of the common myths and misconceptions approximately introversion. It describes how introverts are harassed out in any other case, responding in their precise way to society's stimuli.

The financial disaster additionally explores the phenomenon of "introvert burnout," which happens even as introverts are over stimulated through way of social interactions and discover themselves feeling tired and exhausted. This can bring about a cycle of avoidance and isolation, which could exacerbate emotions of awkwardness and make it even more hard to hook up with others.

Being an introvert also can be a deliver of power and creativity. Introverts frequently have a rich inner worldwide, and can be deeply attuned to their very own mind and emotions. By embracing their particular mind-set, introverts can discover ways to navigate social conditions on their personal terms, and find out high-quality methods to connect with others.

Overall, this monetary break units the diploma for the relaxation of the e book with the useful aid of exploring the complex and regularly difficult enjoy of being an introvert in a international that values extroversion. By acknowledging the worrying conditions and offering techniques for coping, the e-book objectives to help introverts revel in greater assured and snug in social conditions, and in the long run, to thrive of their very very very own specific way.

What is An Introvert?

So, what's an introvert, you ask? Well, permit me can help you understand - it's miles no longer absolutely a elaborate manner of pronouncing "shy" or "anti-social." Introverts are a special breed of those who get their power from solitude and introspection, in desire to from socializing and being the lifestyles of the birthday celebration.

Think people, as like house cats - we love to curve up in our comfy little regions and virtually relax out. And if you strive to pull us out to a noisy bar or celebration, we are going to possibly hiss and scratch at you till you leave us on my own.

But do not worry, it isn't always private. We clearly need our on my own time to recharge our batteries and approach all of the mind and emotions bouncing round in our heads. It's like we've were given a piece inner spa in which we go to meditate and rejuvenate.

Of route, there are a few downsides to being an introvert. We're no longer typically the first rate at small talk or networking, and we are capable of come off as aloof or bored with social situations. But hi there, at the least we're no longer those getting below the influence of alcohol and making fools of ourselves at the company Christmas birthday party, right?

So next time you be conscious an introvert quietly studying a e-book or taking a walk by myself, in reality provide them a short nod of records. We may be an superb breed, but we are no matter the fact that out here, quietly doing our element and gambling our own organization business enterprise.

The Joys of Being an Introvert

Are you an introvert who prefers to spend Friday nights curled up with a tremendous e book instead of navigating the chaos of a crowded bar? Do you dread small talk and awkward social interactions? If so, you are not by myself. Being an introvert can occasionally sense like a burden, however it could additionally be a supply of humor and joy.

For starters, there may be now not something pretty much like the thrill of canceling plans. As an introvert, the possibility of a night time day journey with a massive organization of human beings may experience overwhelming. But even as the ones plans fall through and you get to spend the night time time within the consolation of your own home, it's far natural bliss. No awkward small speak, no stress to be social - just you, your desired pajamas, and a great Netflix binge.

While some humans enjoy the chaos of a packed bar or a live performance, introverts favor to revel in the tranquility in their non-public enterprise. Nothing compares to the delight of curling up with a top notch e book and a warm blanket on a Friday night time, and not using a disturbing distractions or duties. Canceling plans is like hitting the jackpot, except in vicinity of cash, you win the prize of spending the midnight to your comfiest pajamas.

And permit's not forget about the fun of awkward small talk. There's some issue undeniably beautiful about fumbling thru a verbal exchange with a stranger, searching out a few issue - something - to speak about. It's like a recreation of social roulette, with the capacity for recoil-really worth moments at every flip. But whilst we continue to exist these interactions, we emerge stronger and more resilient, organized to tackle the subsequent mission.

Of direction, making new buddies can be a struggle for introverts. It's not that we do not want to connect with others - it's miles actually that the approach may be onerous. Navigating the murky waters of small communicate and searching for common floor with strangers can experience like an Olympic-degree recreation. But whilst we do finally make a actual reference to someone, it is even extra unique.

So certain, being an introvert may be challenging. But it is able to also be appreciably profitable, complete of moments of humor, delight, and surprising connections. So the subsequent time you revel in overwhelmed thru the pressures of social interaction, recollect - there is usually the pride of canceling plans.

The Introvert's Guide to Small Talk: How to Survive Social Events

Ah, small talk - the bane of each introvert's existence. The mere belief of setting up a conversation with a stranger at a social occasion can deliver shivers down our spines. But worry now not, my fellow introverts! With the proper method, you could moreover live on small talk and come out unscathed.

First things first - keep away from talking approximately arguable subjects. Don't point out politics, religion, or the extremely-modern scandalous superstar gossip. Stick to stable subjects, similar to the weather or how delicious the appetizers are.

If you're certainly struggling, attempt working towards your small talk skills with a relied on buddy or family member. Have them fake to be a stranger and practice setting up a conversation. Who is aware about, you would likely even impress them together with your newfound social abilities!

Another seasoned tip - continually have an exit technique. If the communication is dragging on, or in case you're actually now not feeling it, have an excuse ready to head. "Oh, excuse me, I honestly remembered I left my oven on at home" is a conventional and continuously receives the mission accomplished.

And if all else fails, simply be sincere. Tell the person you're talking with that you're not a remarkable deal of a small talker, however you would really like to pay attention greater about their pursuits or pastimes. Who is aware about, you'll probable discover a kindred spirit and make a contemporary pal!

So there you've got it, the introvert's guide to surviving small talk. With a touch education, exercising, and a trusty exit approach, you could moreover navigate social activities like a seasoned. And if all else fails, there can be continuously the comfort of your room to look forward to after the chit chat ends and your favourite ebook is waiting.

The Power of Listening: Why Introverts Make Great Confidants

Well, it's far no thriller that introverts have a unique strength - the energy of listening. They can take a seat quietly for hours, soaking up all of the juicy facts of your existence, without ever interrupting or feeling the want to fill the silence with awkward small communicate.

And permit's be real, who does not love a very good listener? They're like human remedy training, besides with out the hefty fee tag. So, in case you're fortunate enough to have an introvert as your confidant, hold on tight and do not permit bypass. They're an tremendous and valuable breed, and also you do now not need to scare them off alongside facet your loud, extroverted strategies.

But keep in mind, with extraordinary power comes terrific obligation. So, if you're going to spill all your non-public, darkest secrets and techniques and strategies and techniques for your introverted buddy, ensure you convey them a snack or a few aspect. They're going to want a few sustenance to get via all that listening, and also you do not want them passing out on you mid-communique. That's a small price to pay for letting you sell off the heavy burdens that have bothered your thoughts.

So, allow's supply it up for the introverts accessible - the unsung heroes of the confidant international. They might not be the existence of the birthday celebration, but they superb recognize the manner to preserve a secret. And in a worldwide complete of noise, they will be individuals who will pay interest you the loudest.

The Introvert's Dilemma: Balancing Alone Time with Social Obligations

Ah, the traditional introvert's predicament - to socialize or to hibernate like a endure in iciness? It's a tough name, and one which may match away us introverts feeling like we're caught amongst a rock and a tough region. On one hand, we like our on my own time, with our books and our cats and our relaxed blankets. But however, there may be that pesky thing referred to as social responsibilities.

You recognize what I'm speaking about - weddings, occasions, own family gatherings. All the subjects that make us need to move slowly below a rock and in no way come out. It's not that we don't like humans, it's honestly that we need our on my own time like flowers want daylight. Without it, we wither and die (metaphorically speaking, of path).

So, what is an introvert to do? Well, the key is all about stability. You can not spend all of your time on my own, regardless of how tempting that may be. But you moreover mght can't say positive to each social invitation that comes your way, except you want to end up feeling like a tired rag via the give up of the week.

So, right right here's my recommendation: prioritize your social duties, and do now not be afraid to mention no every so often. Choose the events which can be most vital to you and take loads of by myself time to recharge your batteries. And if all else fails, really recollect that you can normally blame it in your cat. "Sorry, I cannot come in your birthday celebration, my cat wishes me." Trust me, it simply works on every occasion.

The Introvert's Inner World: How We Think and Process Information Differently

Ah, the introvert's inner international - a magical region entire of deep mind, complicated emotions, and infinite quantities of overthinking. We introverts might not constantly be the most outwardly expressive humans, but interior our heads is a whole different tale.

While extroverts are to be had dwelling their first-rate lives and making small communicate with all and sundry they meet, we introverts are analyzing each little detail and processing facts on a much deeper degree. We may not commonly be the fastest thinkers, however while we come to a stop, you may bet it's far been very well idea out.

And permit's no longer neglect approximately our overactive imaginations. We introverts can spend hours misplaced in our very non-public thoughts, dreaming up complete worlds and situations that might in no manner even come to fruition. It's each a blessing and a curse, in truth.

But regardless of our introverted quirks, we are regardless of the fact that quite amazing people. Sure, we might also take a hint longer to gadget facts, but as fast as we do, we are a pressure to be reckoned with. So, subsequent time you are putting out with an introvert and they seem misplaced in idea, truely keep in mind - they may be possibly growing with the subsequent splendid concept so as to change the arena. Or they'll be genuinely imagining what it would be need to have a puppy dragon. Either way, it's far all perfect.

Introvert Burnout

Ah, the dreaded introvert burnout. It's like a hangover, but in vicinity of too much booze, it is from too much "people-ing." And let me let you recognise, it's far a actual difficulty.

You understand you're experiencing introvert burnout at the same time as even the perception of socializing makes you want to transport slowly beneath your bed and cover. Your mind looks like a fried egg, your nerves are frayed, and your "human beings tolerance" is at an rock bottom.

But the funny problem approximately introvert burnout is that it often sneaks up on you. You might be feeling pretty extremely good, setting out with a few friends, after which BAM! Your social battery dies, and you're unexpectedly exhausted and cranky.

And then there may be the recovery time. Unlike a normal hangover, that would typically be cured with some greasy meals and a sleep, introvert burnout calls for a greater strategic technique. You also can want a whole day (or week, allow's be actual) to recharge and get again to your normal, introverted self.

So, what is the answer to introvert burnout? Well, you could attempt fending off humans altogether, however it simply is no longer exactly realistic. Instead, you would possibly want to strive setting a few limitations for your self. Don't say certain to each social invitation that comes your manner, and do not be afraid to take breaks sooner or later of social activities to recharge. Blame the bottomless liquids for the frequent visits to the restroom.

And if all else fails, without a doubt tell human beings you have got were given a rare circumstance called "introvertitis" and you need to head domestic and rest. It might not be a real factor, but hi there, occasionally a chunk white lie is the quality manner to live to tell the story on this extroverted international.

Chapter 2: The Art Of Social Distancing

The paintings of social distancing - a knowledge that introverts were running in the direction of for years, long in advance than it have turn out to be a global phenomenon. While the relaxation of the arena is suffering to preserve six toes far from every one-of-a-kind, we introverts are like, "six feet? That's lovable. Try six miles, friend."

But permit's be real—social distancing has its perks. No extra awkward small speak with strangers, no extra crowded sports activities that make us need to run for the hills. We can ultimately include our introverted dispositions without fear of judgment.

And don't even get me commenced on Zoom meetings. As introverts, we were the usage of the "mute" button and hiding our video feeds for years. It's like we have been making prepared for this 2d our whole lives.

Of course, social distancing isn't all rainbows and unicorns. We bypass over our friends and family, and the isolation may be difficult. But for introverts, it is really every other day inside the lifestyles. So, on the identical time because the relaxation of the area is struggling to evolve to this new way of life, we introverts are simply sitting once more, sipping our tea, and pronouncing, "welcome to the club, folks."

The Introvert's Secret Weapon: Social Distancing

Social distancing is the introvert's thriller weapon. While absolutely everyone else is frantically trying to avoid being six ft apart, we introverts were training this artwork for years. It's like we have been education for an epidemic our whole lives. And it's far like introverts anywhere have all of sudden been granted a superpower.

You apprehend what they're saying - "provide an introvert six feet of personal vicinity and they will be happy for an entire life." Okay, possibly no man or woman really says that, however it is actual although.

So, on the equal time as anybody else is freaking out about the pandemic, we introverts are secretly taking detail in our on my own time, sipping tea and studying books inside the consolation of our personal homes. It's like we've got had been given in the end placed our satisfied vicinity. Except, of course, social interactions are slowly returning to pre-pandemic degrees.

How to Avoid Unwanted Social Interactions with Creative Excuses

The artwork of retaining off unwanted social interactions– commonly a undertaking. As introverts, we've got come to be specialists at this. And permit's be real, from time to time the fact virtually may not reduce it. That's wherein cutting-edge excuses are available.

There are such a lot of opportunities right here. You can claim to have an superb sickness that handiest impacts introverts, or that you're honestly an undercover secret agent and you cannot hazard blowing your cover. Or my private preferred - which you're within the witness safety utility and can not display your proper identification.

But why forestall there? You can continuously fake to have a weird hobby that takes up all your free time, like underwater basket weaving or excessive ironing. Or inform them you're in truth schooling for the Olympics and want to consciousness for your recreation.

The key proper right here is to be progressive and convincing. You want to reason them to consider which you definitely cannot come to their occasion, without offending them. It's a sensitive stability, but with sufficient practice, you could turn out to be a seasoned at maintaining off unwanted social interactions.

So the subsequent time you are faced with a social state of affairs you'll as an opportunity keep away from, do no longer in fact say no. Get revolutionary, and who's aware about - you can even enjoy bobbing up with excuses. Just consider, the extra ridiculous, the higher.

The Power of Saying "No" Without Feeling Guilty

The electricity of pronouncing "no" without feeling accountable - a skills that introverts were perfecting for years. We've observed out that now and again, the fantastic way to preserve our treasured by myself time is to surely say "no" to unwanted social interactions.

And allow's be real, pronouncing "no" can be quite empowering. It's like a weight has been lifted off our shoulders, and we will subsequently breathe smooth understanding that we do not ought to perform a little component we do not need to do.

Of route, there are individuals who would likely try to guilt-journey us into pronouncing "positive". But as introverts, we've superior a mystery weapon - the capability to disappear into thin air. We can vanish without a touch, leaving them thinking if we ever even existed in the first area.

And allow's not forget about approximately the revolutionary excuses we are able to provide you with. "Sorry, I should wash my hair that night time" or "I'm allergic to small speak" are conventional examples, but the possibilities are limitless.

So the following time you are confronted with an unwanted social interplay, do not experience guilty about announcing "no". Embrace the strength of your introverted nature and don't forget - sometimes, the incredible manner to attend to yourself is to really say no.

How to Say "No"

Of route you can usually simply shake your head, however in which's the fun in that? Here are greater (and optimistically better) approaches to say no.

1. "I'm sorry, I can not make it. I need to live domestic and rearrange my sock drawer."

2. "I'd like to, but I already made plans to spend the night time speakme to my cat."

three. "No thanks, I even have a warm date with my couch and a exquisite e-book this night time."

4. "Unfortunately, I surely have a preceding engagement with my sweatpants."

5. "Sorry, I can not make it. I ought to reorganize my series of obscure indie films."

6. "I'd love to go back, however my introvert battery is walking low and I want to recharge."

7. "I'm afraid I'll must pass. I even have a urgent engagement with my mind and a cup of tea."

eight. "I cannot make it, sorry. I need to spend the night time thinking of the which means that of life and the universe."

When uncertain, simply say no. It's like a safety net for introverts - a way to guard us from over-committing and sporting out with a social hangover the following day.

Remember, saying "no" is flawlessly ok, although it is not always easy.

Chapter 3: The Joys Of Alone Time

Alone time - the introvert's paradise. While the relaxation of the arena is frantically trying to fill each 2nd with social interplay, we introverts are secretly reveling in the satisfaction of being by myself.

There's some detail magical about the peace and quiet of being with the resource of yourself. No small speak, no obligations, genuinely you and your mind (and probably an exquisite e-book or Netflix binge).

And permit's now not forget approximately the limitless possibilities of what you may do along aspect your by myself time. You can absorb a contemporary interest, like knitting or portray. Or just front room spherical to your pajamas all day, binging on your chosen indicates without fear of judgment.

Of path, some people might probable think that spending too much time on my own is a awful component. But as introverts, we apprehend that being by myself is like recharging our batteries. We want that point to reset and refresh, so we may be our fantastic selves at the equal time as we must interact with others.

So, whilst the relaxation of the arena is constantly searching out new techniques to be social, we introverts are content material to curve up in our favorite chair and bask inside the glory of our on my own time. And genuinely, what may be better than that?

The Introvert's Love for Alone Time and Why It's Important

As an introvert myself, I can attest to the fact that on my own time is sort of a lifeline for us. It's no longer just a preference, it's far a need. We need that point to recharge and system all the data and stimuli we encounter in our each day lives.

Being on my own allows us to completely take satisfaction in our thoughts and feelings without a distractions. It gives us the space to find out our very very own internal worldwide, to reflect on our stories and to benefit a deeper facts of ourselves.

But it is no longer just about introspection - by myself time also lets in us to pursue our passions and hobbies without a outside pressures or interruptions. We can popularity on our hobbies, our modern pursuits, or surely loosen up and recharge our batteries.

And permit's no longer neglect about the importance of placing obstacles. As introverts, we often conflict with feeling like we ought to constantly be "on" for others. But on my own time gives us the possibility to set barriers and deal with ourselves, each mentally and physical.

Plus, allow's be actual - by myself time is in reality easy a laugh. We get to pursue our pastimes, entice up on our favorite indicates, and perhaps even dance throughout the dwelling room like no individual's searching (due to the truth, nicely, no person is).

Sure, some human beings might probably view our love for by myself time as anti-social or bizarre. But as introverts, we understand that it is essential to our nicely-being. Without that point to recharge and refresh, we is probably like a phone with a low battery - continuously getting ready to walking out of juice.

So whilst a few also can view our love for by myself time as anti-social or weird, it's without a doubt a essential part of our nicely-being. It allows us to absolutely encompass and honor our introverted nature, and to be the pleasant model of ourselves - for ourselves and for those spherical us.

The Importance of Scheduling Alone Time in Your Daily Routine

Scheduling on my own time - the introvert's same of scheduling a spa day. It can also sound like a luxurious, however for us introverts, it's miles an absolute necessity.

Without that dedicated time to ourselves, we might be like a plant without water, or a cat without a cardboard area to play in. We'd wither away, or simply start randomly meowing for hobby.

But scheduling by myself time isn't quite a lot self-care - it is about survival. It's about making sure we've the highbrow and emotional area we want to thrive in our every day lives.

So pass ahead and mark that by myself time to your each day planner. Block off an hour or (or 5) handiest for yourself and don't revel in accountable approximately it. Whether it's miles taking a bubble tub, practising yoga, or simply staring off into region, it's far crucial to prioritize your very very own desires and properly-being.

And if every body questions why you're scheduling on my own time, without a doubt tell him or her it is in your very very own sanity. Because permit's be actual - as introverts, our sanity is already putting via a thread.

Party of One: How to Have the Best Time with Your Favorite Person (You)

The sweet bliss of on my own time. No want to make small speak, no want to position on pants, and no need to percentage that closing slice of pizza. In this segment, we can discover the diverse techniques you can have an terrific time along aspect your chosen man or woman: yourself.

"Solo Dance Party: Let Your Inner Beyoncé Shine": Dance! Get your groove on and show yourself what you are fabricated from.

"Movie Night with Me, Myself, and I": No want to argue over what film to have a look at or compromise on snacks. Grab your selected snacks, settle into your coziest spot, and experience a movie night time time with the satisfactory business enterprise: your self.

"Foodie Adventures: Trying New Restaurants Solo": Who dreams a eating companion even as you could attempt out that new sushi region at some stage in using yourself? Enjoy the liberty to reserve some thing you need while no longer having to percentage or make small speak.

"Book Club for One: Discussing Literature with Yourself": Who says e-book clubs need to be social? Have your own ebook membership with your self and speak the modern-day novel with the terrific character to talk to: yourself.

"The Ultimate Self-Care Spa Day": Take an afternoon to pamper your self with a DIY spa day. Indulge in a bubble bath, face mask, and all of the relaxation you want. Plus, no want to share the new bath or pay attention to all of us else's music options.

Remember, being by myself does no longer need to be lonely. It may be a time to connect to yourself and revel in your very own employer. So, permit's increase a tumbler to the closing birthday party of 1!

Introvert Spa Day: Treating Yourself to the Ultimate Solitude Experience

Welcome to Introvert Spa Day, wherein you can experience the ultimate solitude experience!

First, mild some candles and run a bath. Then, spend the following hour silently thinking about the which means of existence, while exfoliating each inch of your body.

Next, take a damage to enjoy a wholesome snack, together with an avocado toast or a kale smoothie. Feel loose to revel in it in complete silence, or have a deep communiqué collectively along with your potted plant.

Now, it is time for a DIY face masks. Apply some yogurt and honey on your face, and permit it sit down down for 20 mins. While geared up, workout some yoga poses or meditate.

Finally, quit the day with a relaxed blanket and an notable eBook. Remember, the final purpose of Introvert Spa Day is to spend extraordinary time collectively together with your favored person - you!

Netflix and Chill (Literally): Binging on Your Favorite Shows Without the Distractions

The joys of Netflix and Chill... Actually As an introvert, there is not something quite like settling in for a marathon of your favored shows, without a distractions or interruptions.

But how are you going to absolutely maximize this experience? Here are a few suggestions:

Create the right viewing surroundings. Set the lighting surely proper, capture your comfiest blanket and pillows, and ensure your snacks are inside arms attain.

Get into man or woman. If you're looking a drama, enjoy loose to dramatically gasp or shout at the display whilst your chosen person meets their lack of existence. If you are looking a comedy, include the laughter and allow those snorts and giggles fly.

Take breaks as wanted. Don't forget about to pause for lavatory breaks, meals refills, or truely to stretch your legs. And if a specific episode hits you proper within the feels, it is okay to take a 2d to build up yourself.

Embrace the strength of the "Next Episode" button. Who desires sleep at the identical time as there may be each other episode simply ready to be watched?

So pass earlier, fellow introverts, take satisfaction in some extreme Netflix and Chill time. Just maintain in mind to go back up for air every sometimes...And probable take a bath.

The Art of Talking to Yourself: Mastering the Inner Monologue

Talking to your self—the simplest communication in which you constantly get to be the expert! But why receive uninteresting self-speak at the same time as you may turn it into an paintings form?

First, pick out out an terrific place. The bathe is continuously a well-known choice; due to the fact the steam gives a dramatic effect for your monologue. But if you really want to channel your inner Shakespeare, try talking to yourself within the the the front of a reflect. Just ensure to check for any lurking roommates or own family folks that would possibly probable mistake your soliloquy for a sign of madness.

Next, pick out a subject. It can be something from a rant approximately your stressful coworker to a philosophical musing on the meaning of existence. Just make certain to preserve it thrilling, so that you do not bore yourself to tears.

And ultimately, do not be afraid to get active. Use hand gestures, change your tone of voice, or even act out scenes in case you're feeling theatrical. Remember, you're the big name of this one-individual show.

With those tips, you may be for your manner to analyzing the artwork of speaking to yourself right away. And who's privy to, maybe sooner or later you may even win an award for your one-individual common performance.

Solitary Adventures: Exploring the World (or Your Own Backyard) on Your Own Terms

The joys of exploring the area to your very personal terms! No waiting for each person else to lure up or compromising on what points of interest to look. In this chapter, we're going to discover the paintings of solitary adventures - from backpacking thru foreign places lands to genuinely taking a stroll through your community.

First things first, you could want to p.C. Your baggage with all of the essentials: a robust backpack, snug footwear, and masses of snacks (due to the truth who's aware of even as the following meals choice will come alongside). And keep in mind your trusty partner - a e-book or podcast to keep you entertained inside the route of any downtime.

Once you're on the road, the possibilities are infinite. Want to spend an entire day exploring a museum or artwork gallery? Go for it. Prefer to spend some time hiking via scenic trails or lounging on the seaside? The preference is yours.

And allow's now not forget about the delivered bonus of touring solo - the freedom to speak to yourself without judgment. Need to schooling session a problem on your head? Just speak it out loud; no individual's around to provide you bizarre appears. Want to sing along for your desired tunes on the top of your lungs? Go in advance, no character's there to pick your questionable track flavor.

So embody the pride of solitary adventures, fellow introverts. Who dreams organisation at the same time as you've got your very very personal outstanding self to discover the area with?

No FOMO Allowed: Embracing the Freedom of Missing Out on Social Events

As introverts, we frequently dread the concept of going out and socializing. But the concern of lacking out (FOMO) can every so often creep in, making us query if we are making the proper preference via staying in.

Well, worry no greater! Embrace the liberty of missing out on social activities with our professional hints:

Remind yourself which you're now not missing out on something except for small communicates and awkward interactions.

Create a faux occasion with a humorous call and inform people you'll that as an alternative. For example, "Sorry, I cannot make it to your party. I even have a meeting with my imaginary friend."

Plan your very own solo celebration collectively collectively with your preferred snacks, movies, and sports. No small communicate required!

Use the time you saved with the aid of the usage of now not attending a social event to do some factor powerful or self-care associated, like organizing your closet or taking a calming bathtub.

When a person asks why you did not attend their occasion, definitely say you've got been too busy being remarkable by myself.

Remember, there may be no disgrace in lacking out on social occasions. As introverts, we thrive in solitude and this is something to be glad with!

The Zen of Silence: Finding Inner Peace within the Absence of Noise and Distractions

Now, let's examine...

Are you bored with consistent noise and distractions? Do you yearn for a second of peace and quiet? Then you, my friend, are inside the right area.

Welcome to "The Zen of Silence," wherein we explore the beauty and advantages of solitude.

Here are some pointers to help you find internal peace within the absence of noise and distractions:

1. Embrace the sound of silence: Instead of seeing silence as an absence of sound, try to understand it as a totally precise sound in and of itself. Listen to the hum of the refrigerator or the rustle of the leaves inside the wind. Bask within the splendor of the quiet.

2. Create your very very very own sanctuary: Whether it's far a nook of your bed room or an entire room dedicated to solitude, ensure it's far an area that makes you experience calm and non violent. Add some vegetation, gentle lighting, and relaxed pillows for maximum rest.

3. Get misplaced in an first rate e-book: Books are the proper break out from the chaos of the out of doors international. Dive right right into a tale and allow yourself wander away in the pages. Bonus elements if it's far a e-book about introverts!

4. Meditate: Meditation is a extremely good manner to clean your thoughts and find out internal peace. Find a comfortable position, close to your eyes, and popularity on your respiration. If your thoughts begins to wander, popularity on your deep breath.

Remember, silence is not the absence of sound; it's far an possibility to connect with your inner self and discover peace. So embody the Zen of Silence and allow it guide you to a greater tranquil and great life.

Chapter 4: The Joys Of Eating Alone

Are you worn-out of having to percent your food or make small talk at the identical time as you eat? Do you crave the peace and quiet of a meal enjoyed solo? Then my fellow introverts, this segment is for you!

The satisfaction of ingesting on my own is a magical experience that mixes the pleasures of meals with the comforts of solitude. Here are a few guidelines to help you encompass this deliciously appealing dependency:

1. Order Exactly What You Want: No need to worry approximately accommodating someone else's taste or dietary regulations. Want a burger with more pickles and a facet of onion earrings? Go for it! Feeling like sushi? Get that highly spiced tuna roll and not the use of a shame.

2. Bring a Book (or Two): Nothing pairs higher with a tasty meal than a fantastic eBook. Lose yourself in a fascinating novel or brush up on your chosen difficulty count number on the

same time as taking element on your food without interruptions.

3. No Sharing Required: Don't you hate it whilst someone takes the last slice of pizza? Or once they want to try your food and grow to be ingesting half of of it? When consuming by myself, there can be no need to percentage, and all of the meals is yours!

4. Dress Code: Who says you have to dress as lots as go out to devour? Eating on my own technique no need for fancy apparel. You can show up to your pajamas in case you need to, no judgment right right here.

five. People Watching: Sometimes the outstanding amusement is certainly searching the arena round you. Find a spot with a terrific view, take a seat down yet again, and experience the display.

6. No Small Talk: One of the great topics about consuming on my own is which you don't need to make small communicate. No want to stress a verbal exchange or fake to be

inquisitive about someone else's story. It's honestly you, your meals, and the peace of mind that consists of it.

So subsequent time you find yourself hungry and in want of some first rate by myself time, keep in mind the satisfaction of eating by myself. Bon appétit!

No Sharing Required: How to Savor Every Bite without Anyone Begging for a Taste

Are you tired of getting to share your meals with others? Do you conceal your plate from hungry fingers begging for a chunk? Fear not, my fellow introverts, for the solution is easy: embody the fun of eating by myself!

When you eat on my own, there can be no want to worry approximately everyone stealing your meals or begging for a taste. You can delight in every delicious chunk without everybody looking for to thieve it away from you. So move in advance, order that greater-huge pizza with all of your chosen toppings and take pleasure in every cheesy, saucy, mouth-watering chunk. No sharing required!

And if you're feeling virtually egocentric, you could even order more than one dishes and characteristic a dinner party all to yourself. Want a steak and lobster tail aggregate? Go for it! Want to try that new vegan burger and fries? Treat yourself, you deserve it.

So the subsequent time you're out to devour and a person attempts to snag a bit from your plate, just bear in mind the amusing of consuming by myself. And in the occasion that they persist, nicely, you can usually inform them the meals's too particularly spiced for their taste.

Table for One, Please: Mastering the Art of Dining Solo

Are you tired of looking in advance to your pals to agree on a eating place or compromising for your selected dishes? Then it's time to recognize the artwork of eating solo, my fellow introverts!

First subjects first, do no longer be afraid to invite for a desk for one. Own it, include it, and enjoy it! And once you have got secured your desk, right here are some recommendations to make the maximum of your solo eating enjoy:

Go Big or Go Home: Order that extra appetizer, dessert, or cocktail without the guilt of sharing or judgment. It's eager on you, and you on my own!

Bring a Good Book: While awaiting your food or savoring each chunk, take satisfaction in a captivating eBook. It's like having a pal with you without the awkward small communicate.

People Watching: Who dreams a date while you may watch the arena bypass via? Observe your environment, wander off to your mind, or strike up a communication collectively collectively with your waiter or waitress. They would possibly just grow to be your new BFF.

Dress Code: Feel free to dress up or down, something makes you experience cushty. No want to have an impact on anyone, simply revel in your very personal corporation.

No Rush: Take some time, revel in the environment, and characteristic fun with every bite. You're not on absolutely everyone else's schedule, so have fun with the immediate.

So, my costly introverted foodies encompass the delight of ingesting solo. You may also moreover even begin to select it over enterprise outings!

No Judgment Zone: Indulging in Your Favorite Foods without Fear of Criticism

Are you bored with feeling chargeable for indulging on your desired food? Do you hate being judged for ordering that second slice of cake or more-massive pizza? Well, my fellow foodie introverts, worry no more! It's time to consist of the No Judgment Zone and experience your food and not using a criticism.

Here are a few tips to help you appreciate every chunk without disgrace:

Order Whatever You Want: Craving a juicy burger with all of the toppings or a bowl of tacky pasta? Go beforehand and order it! Don't permit every person shame you for your food selections.

Eating in Private: Sometimes, you actually need to experience your meals without truly all of us searching. So why no longer sneak off to a quiet nook or your preferred spot within the park and have fun together with your meal in peace?

No Explanation Required: You don't owe each person an cause of your meals selections. Whether you're vegan, vegetarian, or a meat-lover, it's your private choice, and this is all that topics.

Embrace the Leftovers: Who says you cannot have a delicious meal two instances? Embrace the satisfaction of leftovers and enjoy your selected dish again day after today.

Savor Every Bite: Eating on my own way you could make the effort and take pleasure in each bite without everybody rushing you or stealing your food. Enjoy the flavors and textures without a distraction.

Remember, the No Judgment Zone is your sanctuary, and also you need to take pleasure in your favorite meals without fear of grievance. So move in advance, order that greater dessert or massive fries, and revel in each scrumptious chew!

One Plate, No Debate: Making Meal Decisions with Ease

Are you tired of debating with others about in which to eat or what to reserve? Do you want to enjoy a delicious meal with out a compromise or argument? Well, my fellow introverts, you're in authentic fortune because of the reality I've were given a few hints for you.

Welcome to "One Plate, No Debate," the paintings of creating meal choices without troubles.

Here are a few strategies that will help you avoid the again-and-forth of meal making plans:

The Lucky Dip: Write down all your preferred consuming places and meals options on pieces of paper and positioned them in a hat. Let destiny decide wherein and what you may consume today.

The Solo Survey: When eating on my own, you get to select the whole lot and no longer using a objections. So why now not conduct a quick survey of yourself? Ask yourself what you're within the temper for and go along with the number one answer that involves mind. You won't remorse it.

The Food Roulette: Feeling adventurous? Let your taste buds guide you. Close your eyes, spin round, and prevent anywhere you land.

The closest eating place or food stand can be your destination for the day.

The Wildcard: If you enjoy extra ambitious, allow someone else decide for you. Find a chum, family member, or perhaps a stranger, and ask them to choose out out in which and what you may consume. Who is privy to, you may discover a contemporary favored dish or eating place.

So, there you have have been given it, my fellow introverts. With the ones guidelines, you may make meal alternatives successfully and without a debate. Enjoy your food without any compromise or negotiation!

The Solitude of the Solo Meal: Embracing Dining Alone as an Introvert

Have you ever determined yourself at a night meal with a plate of meals in front of you, desperately trying to consider some aspect to say to the individual sitting next to you? Meanwhile, all you actually need to do is enjoy your food in silence? Well, worry no longer! "The Sound of Silence: Enjoying Your Food without the Pressure of Small Talk" is right right right here to maintain the day (and your urge for meals).

Imagine a international wherein you can get pride from every chunk of your meal without having to engage in awkward small communicate approximately the weather or your weekend plans. A global wherein you can absolutely take a seat lower lower back, loosen up, and allow the sound of your chewing fill the room. Sounds like heaven, does not it?

With "The Sound of Silence," you may eventually smash loose from the social obligations of mealtime communiqué and encompass the joy of eating in peace. No greater forced smiles or fake laughs, absolutely you and your meals, dwelling your satisfactory lives.

So pass earlier, take a piece, and experience the sweet sound of silence. Your flavor buds (and your sanity) will thanks.

Chapter 5: Why Introverts Need A Break Day Even From Their Specific Someone

Ah, introverts. They're like unicorns - unusual, mysterious, and sometimes a chunk cranky.

You see, introverts are like batteries. They need to recharge their social energy from time to time, or they'll start to enjoy worn-out and beaten. And let's face it, even the most precise of someone's can be a piece of a drain on your energy tiers.

So, in case you're an introvert in a dating, it's miles essential to take a break each from time to time. And no, I do not advise in reality hiding within the lavatory for a few minutes. I'm speak me a whole-on "I'm going to spend the day studying in my pajamas" shape of damage.

Now, I comprehend what you are wondering - "But may not my specific someone miss me?" Well, of route they may. But reflect onconsideration on it this manner: absence makes the coronary coronary heart broaden fonder. Plus, who is aware of? Maybe they may revel in the harm from your introverted techniques and spend the day doing their own detail.

So drift ahead, introverts, take that well-deserved damage. Your unique someone will recognize. And within the event that they do no longer, properly...You can also normally blame it in your introverted nature.

The Challenges of Maintaining Boundaries in a Relationship

Being in a courting is like gambling a recreation of tug-of-struggle, besides in desire to a rope, you're pulling on every other's feelings. And as an introvert, it can be in particular difficult to hold barriers at the same time as your accomplice's emotional tug feels more like a big tractor pulling you out of your relaxed introvert cave.

It's like seeking to bring together a wall around yourself to maintain your electricity degrees intact; however your accomplice maintains searching out to poke holes in it with their emotional neediness. And let's face it, occasionally their emotional neediness feels greater like a black hollow sucking you in.

But fear no longer, introverts! You can maintain your barriers and keep your companion glad at the identical time. It's all approximately locating the proper stability, like a touchy dance amongst your want for by myself time and their want for affection.

Just consider, verbal exchange is top. So even as your accomplice is tugging to your emotional rope a piece too tough, don't be afraid to talk up and say, "Hey, I want some by myself time to recharge my introverted batteries. Can we plan a few by myself time for later?"

And if all else fails, honestly remind your companion that you're like a cat - you adore them, but now and again you virtually want to cover below the mattress and take a nap.

Balancing Quality Time with Personal Time

Being in a relationship is like having a 2d full-time venture, besides the pay is terrible and the simplest advantages are occasional cuddles and emotional guide. And as an introvert, it can be even extra difficult to juggle the desires of a courting even as also looking for time for yourself.

It's like trying to stability a plate of spaghetti in your nose while using a unicycle. Sure, it's miles viable, however it is not exactly cushty or sustainable.

You can find out that perfect balance among fantastic time collectively collectively with your partner and private time to recharge. It's all approximately scheduling, conversation, and a piece of compromise.

Just undergo in mind, private time is like your mystery stash of chocolate - you do not need to percentage it with absolutely everyone (no longer even your partner). So when they propose a romantic date night time time time within the path of your personal time, do now not be afraid to say, "Sorry, love, I have already got plans to binge-watch my favourite display in my PJs this night time."

And in case your associate wishes a touch extra interest, just remind them you are like a plant - you need each sunshine and on my own time to thrive. So move in advance, bask in the daylight of your associate's affection, but take into account to make the effort to enlarge and recharge for your personal.

Avoiding Burnout and Resentment in a Relationship

Being in a dating is like strolling a marathon, except in area of a stop line; you are virtually looking for to avoid getting burnt out and resentful. And as an introvert, it may be mainly tough to keep your strength stages up at the same time as additionally meeting your partner's goals.

It's like seeking to preserve a fire burning without adding any gasoline - in the long run, you will run out of power and feel burnt out. And permit's now not forget about about about the resentment that may building up while you sense you're giving greater than you are becoming.

But worry no longer, introverts! You can avoid burnout and resentment to your dating with a few easy hints. It's all approximately setting barriers, pronouncing "no" while you want to, and locating innovative strategies to recharge your introverted batteries.

Just recall, it's miles k to say "no" in your companion's requests for interest or affection. Sometimes you want to prioritize your personal desires and say, "Sorry, love, I can not come on your cousin's 1/three wedding this month. I want some time to recharge my batteries."

And if you're feeling burnt out and envious, truely remind your accomplice that you are like a rechargeable battery - you need time to rest and recharge earlier than you can provide your all another time. So move earlier, take that lengthy bubble tub, take a look at that e book you've got were given been looking to look at, or spend a few amazing time collectively together with your puppy rock. Your introverted batteries will thank you.

Communicating Needs and Boundaries in a Relationship

Being in a courting is like playing a recreation of cell phone, besides in vicinity of whispering phrases; you are trying to speak your needs and limitations for your partner. And as an introvert, it could be particularly tough to discover the right phrases to say without feeling like you're over-sharing or under-sharing.

It's like trying to play charades in a remote places language - super, you could gesture and make sounds, however your partner won't understand what you are trying to mention. And permit's now not forget approximately approximately the awkwardness of looking to communicate your needs without sounding like a needy introvert.

Yet, you may talk your desires and obstacles to your dating without feeling like an entire weirdo. It's all about locating the right stability among honesty and international members of the family.

Just don't forget, honesty is the terrific insurance - but from time to time a bit white lie can circulate a protracted manner. So at the same time as your associate asks if you want to go to their own family reunion, do now not be afraid to say, "Sorry, love, I can not make it this one year. I actually have an critical assembly with my cat."

And in case you're struggling to find out the proper terms to talk your wishes and barriers, simply remind your accomplice that you are like a e-book - you have got had been given a variety of interesting things to say, however now and again you want a chunk quiet time to accumulate your thoughts. So circulate beforehand, take the time to think about what you need to mention, and while you are prepared, speak your desires and boundaries with self notion (and perhaps a piece of humor).

Activities for Introverts to Recharge Alone

Being an introvert is like being a superhero, besides in desire to combating crime, you're preventing the urge to strangle human beings for speak me too much. And at the equal time as you want to recharge your introverted batteries, it's hard to find the proper sports activities that permit you to recharge by myself.

It's like looking for a needle in a haystack - best, there are hundreds of factors to do, however locating the right interest that permits you to recharge and avoid human interplay may be a challenge.

But of course there are masses of sports activities sports you could do to recharge by myself without feeling accountable or bored.

It's all about finding what works for you and embracing your internal introvert.

Just bear in mind, by myself time is form of a spa day in your soul - it's far critical to deal with yourself every so often. So go earlier, take pride in your preferred interests, like knitting, reading, or looking paint dry.

And if you're feeling in particular adventurous, try a few new sports activities that will let you recharge by myself, like taking a solo hike inside the woods, or on the lookout for to construct a birdhouse without a human interplay.

Just recall, the crucial thing to recharging as an introvert is to embody your on my own time and prioritize your own wishes. So pass beforehand, be your introverted self and recharge your batteries. You'll sense like a superhero another time right away!

Chapter 6: How To Survive Parties

What do introverts hate about events? The loud tune, the chatty strangers, the compulsory small communicate - it's far enough to make us need to move slowly proper into a hollow and in no way come out.

It may be complex, but there are methods to continue to exist occasions without losing our minds (or our dignity). From strategically choosing our seating preparations to pretending we've got got an urgent cell phone call, we have got have been given this party survival hassle all the way down to a technological information.

And allow's not forget about our mystery weapon - the Irish good-bye. Sneaking out of a celebration without pronouncing goodbye to anyone may additionally moreover seem impolite to a few, but for us introverts, it's far the final act of self-renovation.

Parties: The Introvert's Worst Nightmare

Parties - One phrase, multiple opportunities, most of them cringey for introverts. It's the get collectively that moves fear into the hearts of folks who favor to spend their evenings curled up with a superb e-book. The idea of creating small talk with strangers, undertaking compelled communication and seeking to appear "cool" is enough to make an introvert escape in hives.

For an introvert, a celebration is sort of a recreation of Russian Roulette - you in no way realize on the equal time as you'll be cornered via the usage of that one man or woman who desires to talk to you about their cat for hours on cease. And don't even get me started out at the horrifying celebration video video video games. When the tune starts off evolved off evolved and the organization starts off evolved to dance, the introvert is left thinking if it's miles socially ideal to simply sit down down inside the nook and watch.

Yet, there may be a manner to live to inform the story the ones social situations. It entails locating the closest snack table and quietly munching away on the same time as pretending to be engrossed inside the dips. And if that does not paintings, there's always the toilet - a sanctuary for the ones in need of a ruin from the social chaos.

So, subsequent time you are invited to a celebration, preserve in thoughts - it can be your worst nightmare, however with a piece of creativity and pretty a few snacks, you could live on. And who's aware about, you can even discover a kindred spirit hiding in the nook, seeking to keep away from eye touch with the extroverts at the dance floor.

Tips for Surviving Social Gatherings

Social gatherings can be overwhelming, particularly for introverts. Fortunately, there are recommendations and tricks to surviving the ones activities without losing your mind. Here are some of the satisfactory ones:

1. Arrive fashionably overdue: Show as lots because the birthday party a touch later than

all and sundry else. That way, you could pass the awkward small communicate and pass right now to the snacks.

2. Find a quiet corner: Scope out a quiet nook wherein you may hide and check the party from a distance. It's like gambling Where's Waldo, however with people as opposed to a person in a striped blouse.

3. Have an go out technique: Always have an excuse organized to depart early. "Oh no, my puppy rock wants to be fed" is a traditional. And if all else fails, truly say you have were given an top notch clinical situation that calls so that it will sleep for 18 hours a day.

4. Bring a plus one: If you're truly dreading the party, deliver a friend or big distinct who can be your buffer. Bonus factors if they'll be outgoing and might manipulate all of the small communicate.

5. Fake it 'til you're making it: If all else fails, really fake to be an extrovert. Smile, nod, and say "wow" loads. People will think you're

listening, even in case you're in reality virtually thinking about what you may devour next.

With the ones guidelines, you may be capable of live on any party. And who is aware about, you may even have an exquisite time! Just keep in mind to tempo yourself at the snacks,

How to Politely Decline Invitations without Hurting Anyone's Feelings

It's a challenge; however you can with courtesy decline invitations without hurting anyone's feelings. You can use humor for one issue.

Here are some excuses you can use:

Step 1: Develop a fake hypersensitive reaction to the entirety.

Step 2: When a person invites you to some issue, say, "Oh, I'd want to, however I'm allergic to [insert activity here]." If it's far a night meal, say you're allergic to the whole thing on the menu. If it's miles a movie night time time, say you are allergic to popcorn. And in the long run, if it's miles a karaoke night, say you are allergic to bad creating a music.

Step 3: If someone catches on in your fake allergic reaction, transfer it up and say you are allergic to a few thing else. For example, "Oh, I apprehend I said I turn out to be allergic to karaoke, but it appears I'm additionally allergic to mini-golfing."

Step four: Blame your imaginary twin. "I'm sorry; I can't make it on your celebration. My dual brother/sister is journeying from out of metropolis and I promised to show them round."

Step five: If none of those excuses work, truly be honest and inform them you cannot make it. But make certain to function a bit humor to melt the blow. "I'm sorry; I can't make it for your paint and sip birthday party. I'm afraid I might also emerge as sipping the paint as an alternative."

Remember, it's far important to be kind and thoughtful at the same time as declining invitations, even in case you're using humor to do it. After all, no person likes a party pooper.

Chapter 7: The Art Of Small Talk For Introverts

Introverts, have a laugh! You not ought to undergo via painful small talk with strangers or friends. With a chunk of exercise, you can also hold close the art work of small speak without feeling like you are death internal.

Here are a number of the stairs in making small communicate:

1. Establish eye contact without staring intensely, only a quick look is enough.

2. Use a grin to make the opportunity individual feel comfortable.

3. Start the communication with anything, even something easy like "Hey, how's it going?"

4. Pay interest and actively be aware of the possibility person, ask them inquiries to encourage them to speak approximately themselves.

5. Follow up on what they are announcing, asking greater questions about interesting topics or finding a manner to narrate to mundane ones.

By following those five steps, you may beautify your small speak competencies. Even if you experience like you're suffering, maintaining a pleasing demeanor and displaying hobby in what the alternative person is saying can bypass a long manner in making them experience comfortable and engaged inside the communiqué.

Embracing Silence

As introverts, silence is our fine buddy. It's a region wherein we are able to recharge our batteries, approach our thoughts, and actually exist in peace.

In a society full of noise, here are guidelines on a manner to include the silence:

1. Schedule time for silence: Set apart a few minutes each day to be in silence. Whether it's far inside the morning, within the course

of a damage, or earlier than bed, use this time to mirror, meditate, or clearly be gift together collectively with your mind.

2. Engage in mindfulness: Being aware and without a doubt gift within the second can be a effective manner to encompass silence. Focus for your breath, environment, or body to quiet your mind and embody the stillness.

3. Disconnect from technology: In a worldwide this is continuously related, locating silence can be a assignment. Try taking a destroy from generation, which incorporates turning off your smartphone or laptop for some hours each day, to create region for silence.

4. Connect with nature: Nature can provide a non violent surroundings for embracing silence. Take a stroll within the woods, sit down down with the beneficial aid of a circulation, or gaze at the celebrities to locate tranquility. Reflect on yourself: Use silence as a time for self-reflected photograph. Think about your values, goals, and priorities, which

can help you discover readability and path for your existence. Remember to embody mindfulness and self-reflected photograph as effective gadget for discovering the splendor of silence.

Finding Common Ground: Tips for Identifying Shared Interests

Breaking the ice and finding not unusual ground with a person you've got in reality met may be pretty a undertaking. But fear no longer, for we have got got a few pointers with the intention to can help you understand shared pursuits and maintain the verbal exchange flowing easily:

Start with Compliments. If you be aware something exciting or precise approximately the other man or woman, deliver them a actual reward. Not most effective will it lead them to enjoy right, however it could furthermore offer you with insights into their tastes and options.

Ask Open-Ended Questions. Avoid clean certain-or-no questions and as an alternative, ask questions that encourage the opposite man or woman to proportion more about themselves. For instance, as opposed to asking "Do you need sports activities activities sports?" strive asking, "What's your chosen game to study or play?"

Use Your Environment. If you're at an event or in a selected placing, use your surroundings as a communiqué starter. For example, in case you're at a park, you may ask the other character if they arrive right proper right here frequently or what their desired outdoor interest is.

With these suggestions in mind, you will be capable of discover not unusual floor and hook up with strangers like a pro. And if all else fails, just consider that everyone loves pizza - it is a confident communication starter!

Breaking the Ice: Strategies for Starting a Conversation

Breaking the ice may be tougher than trying to break open a coconut with a toothpick; I've have been given some hilarious strategies to help you out!

1. Make a comedian tale - "Why changed into the mathematics eBook sad? Because it had too many troubles."

2. Talk about a few element uncommon - "Did you apprehend that a group of flamingos is referred to as a flamboyance?"

3. Ask them a stupid query - "If you can have any superpower, what might not it be?"

4. Introduce yourself with a playful nickname. For example, "Hey there, I'm the Taco Whisperer. What's your call?"

5. Give them a honest praise which you genuinely endorse. It can be a smile, a fashion revel in. Anything as long as it's miles genuine.

Remember, it is definitely super to be a bit goofy and characteristic a few a laugh whilst you're trying to break the ice. You by no means apprehend, your playful technique may additionally additionally certainly enliven their day!

Navigating Awkward Silences: Techniques for Keeping the Conversation Going

Navigating awkward silences may be more tough than attempting to walk on a tightrope at the same time as juggling pineapples, but don't worry; I've were given a few techniques to help you hold the communiqué going!

1. Break the silence with a noisy, exaggerated yawn and say, "Sorry, I did no longer sleep well final night time. Do you recognize any right bedtime testimonies?"

2. Pull out your cellphone and show them a hilarious meme or video, saying, "I'm quite positive this is what the Internet have emerge as made for!"

3. Make up a daft tale about a fictional character, like a ninja unicorn who saves the area from a large marshmallow monster.

4. Ask them to play a sport of "Would You Rather?" and offer you with absurd situations, like "Would you as an alternative have a puppy elephant or a pet giraffe?"

5. Offer to do a silly venture, like seeing who could make the most bizarre noise with their mouth.

6. Ask open-ended questions - "What's the most interesting detail you've completed this 365 days?" This encourages the opportunity individual to share more and can bring about a extra appealing communication. And then you can tell them approximately your domestic dog goldfish.

7. Share a tale - "Did I ever inform you about the time I with the resource of chance locked myself out of my residence?" Sharing a non-public story can help ruin the tension and supply the opportunity man or woman a few difficulty to relate to.

8. Find a few thing in commonplace - "I observed you are sporting a band t-shirt, do

you want going to stay suggests?" This will let you each discover a few issue to connect on and talk about.

Remember, navigating awkward silences may be awkward in itself, so do not be afraid to add a chunk humor and maintain matters moderate-hearted!

The Power of Listening: How to Be a Good Listener and Build Connections

The electricity of listening is similar to the power of an terrific pair of noise-canceling headphones - it can block out all the distractions and assist you gather real connections with humans. Here are some hilarious guidelines to help you be a remarkable listener:

1. Pretend to be a parrot and repeat everything they may be saying decrease decrease again to them. "Wow, that's truly interesting! So, you are saying that you could talk fluent whale?"

2. Nod your head lots which you appear to be a bobble head doll, and say "Mmm-hmm" each few seconds. This will display them you're paying hobby and furthermore supply them a superb snort.

3. Use exaggerated facial expressions to reveal them you're surely listening, like widening your eyes or gasping dramatically. Bonus factors in case you throw in a few "oh nos!" and "oh mans!"

4. Take notes on everything they may be saying and act like a detective who's looking to treatment a thriller. "Interesting, so you say you need pineapple to your pizza. Do you actually have a thriller love for anchovies?"

Remember, being an extremely good listener does not ought to be stupid! Have fun with it and show your silly element. Who is aware of, you could surely make their day collectively together with your comedic method!

Asking the Right Questions: Techniques for Showing Interest and Curiosity

Asking the right questions is like gambling a undertaking of 20 questions - besides you do now not need to emerge as asking, "Is it a rock?" Here are a few hilarious techniques to expose interest and hobby:

1. Start every query with "In a international in which..." to make it sound extra epic."In a global where cats can speak, what do you believe you studied your cat might say?"

2. Ask them a question that has now not something to do with the conversation, like "Do you trust in extraterrestrial beings? Because I saw a UFO closing night time and I need a person to another time me up!"

3. Make a assertion disguised as a query, like "You appear like someone who is clearly well at juggling flamingos. Am I proper?"

4. Ask them a hypothetical question it is so absurd, it'll motive them to chortle. "If you could have any superpower, however it had to be genuinely vain, what could no longer it is?"

5. Ask them a question that you already realize the answer to, without a doubt to debris with them. "So, I heard you're secretly a ninja. Is that real?"

Remember, asking the proper questions don't should be a essential rely. Have a laugh with it and show your silly facet! You in no manner comprehend; you will likely just spark a hilarious communication that they'll preserve in thoughts for years yet to come.

Exiting Gracefully: Strategies for Ending Conversations Politely

Exiting a conversation gracefully is like looking to depart a party without absolutely every person noticing - it could be complicated, however with those hilarious techniques, you will be a seasoned!

1. Suddenly soar up and say, "Oh no, I absolutely remembered, I left my domestic dog llama in the oven! Gotta move!"

2. Pull out a faux cellphone and say, "Sorry, I have to take this call. It's my imaginary pal, and he is in a catastrophe!"

3. Act together with you virtually remembered something urgent and say, "Excuse me, I should pass seize a bus to my alien planet. See you later!"

4. Suddenly start doing the Macarena dance and say, "Oops, sorry, it's miles a reflex. Gotta pass, I promised I'd perform for the President."

5. Simply say, "It's been tremendous speaking to you; however I should circulate feed my domestic dog rock now. He's on a strict weight loss plan."

Remember, exiting a communication gracefully does not need to be a excessive rely quantity number. Have fun with it and display your stupid facet! Who is aware of, you will probable without a doubt cause them to chuckle and give up the conversation on a immoderate phrase.

Chapter 8: Finding Your Tribe

Yes, you'd choose to be by myself, but every now and then it's right to recognize that there are like-minded people. And it's commonly a super idea to be part of a tribe.

1. finding your tribe is like seeking to collect a squad for a heist - but rather than robbing a financial group, you're actually attempting to devise the appropriate brunch.

2. it's like assembling your personal non-public Avengers crew, but in area of stopping Thanos, the most effective stones you're inquisitive about are jackstones.

3. It's like seeking to build a fixed for a fact show, but rather than competing for a cash prize, you are virtually searching for to make a few lifelong buddies and have a blast along the way.

4. it's like a select-your-very own-journey e-book in which you're simply searching out folks that love puns and terrible jokes.

5. Its like accumulating Funko Pop figures, but as an alternative, you are accumulating people with unique personalities and hobbies.

Remember, locating your tribe would not must be a excessive count quantity. Have a laugh with it and show your silly aspect! Who is aware of, you will possibly absolutely enchantment to three exceptional people who come to be lifelong buddies.

The Introvert's Struggle to Find Like-minded People

Introverts often locate it hard to find like-minded people due to the fact they choose smaller social circles and similarly intimate interactions. Here are a few takes at the introvert's warfare to find their tribe:

1. Trying to discover your tribe as an introvert is like seeking out a needle in a haystack, besides the needle is a set of folks who determine on reading books to developing small communicate.

2. it's like looking for a unicorn - you recognize they exist, however they may be elusive and difficult to return via.

3. it's like attempting to find a quiet corner in a noisy birthday celebration - you have to navigate thru the sea of people and noise to discover your tribe.

4. It's like trying to find a exceptional Wi-Fi connection in a far off area - you need to go looking immoderate and low, or maybe then, it might not be strong enough to attach.

5. It's like searching out a parking spot at a crowded mall within the route of the holidays - you want to circle round for hours, and surely whilst you anticipate you have decided a gap, someone else swoops in and takes it.

6. Trying to discover your tribe as an introvert is like attempting to find Waldo in a crowded stadium - he is there someplace, but it takes severa patience and attempt to perceive him.

7. it's like gambling a activity of cover and are searching for for, but rather than hiding in

the back of wooden and timber, your tribe is hiding in libraries, espresso shops, and bookstores.

8. It's like trying to find an outstanding Pokémon within the wild, but in place of a Pikachu, you're searching for a set of folks who proportion your love of introversion and recognize your quiet nature.

9. it's like attempting to find an identical sock in a pile of laundry - you apprehend it's there someplace, but it's miles buried underneath a pile of mismatched and loud socks.

Remember, notwithstanding the reality that locating like-minded people can be a conflict for introverts, it isn't not possible. With a bit of staying strength and perseverance, you may locate your tribe and feature a fantastic time with them.

Tips for Finding Your Tribe

Here are a few hints to find out your tribe.

1. Join a knitting membership - it's far like finding a needle in a haystack, but in vicinity of a needle, you will discover a business enterprise of like-minded those who love yarn and snug sweaters.

2. Take a cooking splendor - it is a terrific way to satisfy human beings and provoke your future night meal site visitors together with your newfound culinary capabilities.

3. Join a e-book club - because of the reality what's higher than discussing the modern-day-day bestseller with a tough and fast of bookworms? Just ensure to surely have a take a look at the e-book earlier than the meeting!

4. Take up a modern hobby - who knows, you could find out a hidden expertise for pottery or macramé, and meet a few extraordinary people along the way.

5. Join a wine-tasting agency - because of the fact no longer anything brings people together like a superb glass of wine. Plus, you

may examine a factor or about vintages and varietals.

Remember, finding your tribe is all approximately exploring your pursuits and passions, and connecting with like-minded human beings. So go in advance and attempt something new, you by no means realise who you'll probably meet!

How to Make Friends Without Leaving Your Comfort Zone

Here are a few humorous hints on a way to make buddies without leaving your comfort area:

1. Start a virtual e book membership - due to the reality discussing your selected books from the comfort of your private home is the final introvert dream.

2. Join a web gaming community - due to the fact not anything says friendship like bonding

over a shared love of World of War craft or Animal Crossing.

3. Attend digital networking activities - due to the truth who dreams small communicate at the same time as you may talk hold with like-minded specialists from the consolation of your non-public sofa?

4. Join a Face book organization in your preferred TV show - because of the fact not anything brings people collectively like a shared obsession with Game of Thrones or The Office.

5. Take up an internet direction - because of the truth learning cutting-edge-day skills is constantly a extraordinary conversation starter, and you will likely really discover your destiny amazing friend in the statement segment.

Remember, making buddies could no longer have to be an extrovert's exercise. Embrace your inner introvert and find strategies to connect to humans from the comfort of your own home. Who is aware of, you will in all likelihood sincerely make a few fantastic friends without ever having to area on pants.

Chapter 9: The Introvert As A Romance Partner

Falling in love with an introvert may be a completely particular and profitable enjoy. While introverts are often misunderstood and can be seen as shy or reserved, they own many functions that would make them pleasant partners. They display love thru thoughtful gestures, determine upon low-key romance, and might not name for everyday hobby or stimulation. Introverts are fantastic listeners, introspective, dependable and dedicated, independent, and often cutting-edge. They offer a deep and amazing connection this is well well well really worth the attempt.

The Art of Low-Key Romance

Introverts are the masters of the art work of low-key romance. We realize the way to set the temper with out going overboard - assume candlelit dinners at domestic, snug film nights, and long walks beneath the celebrities. We're now not the sort to make grand gestures or placed on a big show, but we're going to reveal you like in our own quiet way.

We're all about the small topics that make a huge impact, like leaving you a sweet look at to find in your pocket, unexpected you alongside side your chosen deal with, or searching after something you've got been getting rid of. We comprehend that it's miles the little matters that depend, and we are happy to place inside the attempt to make you enjoy loved and favored.

Of direction, we furthermore realize the way to spice subjects up when the temper movements. We're no longer afraid to try new subjects or find out our passions, but we're going to do it in a way that is comfortable and actual to us. Whether it is making an attempt a new recipe collectively or taking a weekend journey to a comfy cabin in the woods, we're going to ensure that the revel in is significant and amazing.

So in case you're seeking out a accomplice who is aware of a way to convey the romance without going overboard, look no further than an introvert. We might not be the flashiest or most extroverted, but we are able to make certain that you're feeling cherished and loved in our very personal quiet way.

Why Silence is Important in Relationships

When you are dating an introvert, silence is not without a doubt golden - it is herbal platinum. We're not the sort to fill every second with chatter or noise, and we are flawlessly happy to take a seat down in snug silence. In truth, now and again silence may be the maximum romantic element of all.

While terrific couples may also enjoy the need to fill each second with communication or pastime, introverts are happy to absolutely be collectively in quiet companionship. We do no longer need to fill the air with phrases or noise - we're content cloth cloth to genuinely exist inside the same place and enjoy each awesome's enterprise company.

Of path, it virtually is not to mention that we do now not enjoy verbal exchange or communique. We clearly pick out to do it in our very private way and on our very private terms. We may not be the maximum vocal or expressive, but we're going to show you like and affection in our very own quiet way.

So if you're courting an introvert, do now not be fearful of silence. Embrace it, get pride from it, and enjoy it. Because when you're with an introvert, every now and then the most romantic moments are the ones in that you don't say a phrase.

The One-on-One Connection

When it comes to dating introverts, overlook approximately huge businesses or crowded sports - the only-on-one connection is in which it is at. Introverts thrive on deep, extensive conversations and private connections, and there may be nothing we adore greater than analyzing a person on a one-on-one diploma.

While extroverts might probably revel in the a laugh of a large party, introverts favor to hobby on the person they'll be with and actually get to realise them on a deeper diploma. We're not the kind to jump from person to individual or communique to verbal exchange - we're all about that one-on-one connection.

And while we connect to someone, we definitely commit. We're now not interested in superficial relationships or casual flings - we need a few issue right. So if you're relationship an introvert, be prepared for some excessive one-on-one time.

Of path, that does not imply we're now not up for a few amusing and journey. We truely select to do it in a way it's more intimate and personal. Maybe it's miles a cushty night time in with a notable movie, a romantic dinner for two, or a protracted stroll beneath the celebs - some issue it's miles, we are going to make certain that it is huge and noteworthy.

So in case you're seeking out a partner who's all approximately that one-on-one connection, appearance no in addition than an introvert. We won't be the lifestyles of the party, however we are able to provide you with our entire interest and connect with you on a degree this is deep, significant, and oh-so-romantic.

xQuality Over Quantity

When it involves relationship introverts, it is all about fine over amount. We're not inquisitive about gambling the numbers undertaking or racking up a protracted list of romantic conquests - we need some thing real, significant, and lasting.

While an prolonged listing of dates or a packed social calendar may probable provoke a few humans, introverts understand the ones topics do no longer constantly cause real happiness or fulfillment. Instead, we pick to awareness on constructing robust, deep connections with the humans we care approximately.

We're now not interested by shallow relationships or fleeting connections. We want to invest our time and power into people who in reality rely range to us, and we're inclined to study for the proper character to go back decrease back along.

Of course, that does not suggest we're no longer up for a few amusing and journey. We clearly choose to do it in a way it's miles significant and enjoyable. Maybe it's far a quiet night time in with a excellent e-book, a deep communication over a cup of coffee, or a hike inside the incredible outdoors - a few component it is, we can make certain that it's a terrific experience.

So in case you're searching out a companion who's all about wonderful over amount, appearance no in addition than an introvert. We may not have a packed social calendar, however we can come up with our entire interest and construct a deep, meaningful connection an exquisite manner to remaining an entire lifestyles.

Date Night In

Introverts as romance companions often excel at "Date Night In" due to the fact they do no longer need to depart the consolation in their personal home to experience loved and desired. Plus, they can keep away from the problem of putting on pants!

For introverts, an outstanding "Date Night In" can also involve cuddling up on the sofa with an first-rate book or film, cooking a scrumptious meal together, or carrying out a shared hobby or hobby. Who wishes a fancy eating place or crowded bar even as you could have all the a laugh and romance of a date night time time from the comfort of your non-public residing room?

And permit's be actual, introverts have been working in the direction of social distancing prolonged before it have become cool. So, in case you're searching out a partner who is aware of a manner to hold subjects cushty, low-key, and strain-loose, look no similarly than your wonderful network introvert.

So, grasp a few snacks, located for your comfiest pajamas, and settle in for a night of love, laughter, and perhaps a bit of Netflix and kick back. With an introvert with the resource of your aspect, you're confident to have a date night to recall (or probably just a date night to forget due to the truth you fell asleep at the sofa).

The Master of the Slow Burn

The Slow Burn - the introvert's manner to steamy romance. While some may additionally select the fast and easy technique to like, introverts realize that right matters come to people who wait, and that consists of romance.

As the Master of the Slow Burn, introverts recognize that the satisfactory relationships are built on a basis of remember, records, and endurance. They realize that love is a marathon, now not a sprint, and that taking the time to clearly get to understand someone can motive a deeper and extra significant connection.

While a few also can view introverts as being slow to open up or hesitant to make the first bypass, it's miles all a part of their strategic plan to win your coronary heart. They may additionally take a touch longer to warmth as a whole lot as you, but when they do, they're all in, and their commitment and loyalty will in no way waver.

Plus, the Master of the Slow Burn is aware about that anticipation may be a powerful aphrodisiac. They may additionally deliver you a thoughtful textual content message or leave you a surprise phrase, slowly constructing up the tension and satisfaction till the on the spot is simply right.

So, in case you're seeking out a partner who is aware of the fee of staying strength, who is aware of that authentic matters come to people who wait, and who can turn up the heat with a single look, look no further than the introvert - the Master of the Slow Burn.

The Bookish Babe/Bro

The Bookish Babe/Bro - the introvert's best in form. When it consists of romance, there may be not anything sexier than a person who is aware of their manner round an incredible ebook.

For introverts, the Bookish Babe/Bro is the proper accomplice - a person who is aware the importance of quiet time, considerate reflected photo, and an notable cup of tea. They can also moreover spend hours out of place in a unique, but after they emerge, they may have masses of insights and reviews to percent.

And allow's be real, introverts love an notable communication accomplice, and the Bookish Babe/Bro in no way disappoints. They're continuously up for a lively debate, a deep dive into a topic of interest, or a shared appreciation for a specific author or fashion.

Plus, there can be some thing undeniably appealing approximately someone who's properly-take a look at and informed approximately the arena round them. The

Bookish Babe/Bro has a revel in of intellectual hobby and a desire for self-improvement this is each inspiring and attractive.

So, in case you're looking for a partner who is aware of their way round a library, who can maintain you engaged and entertained for hours, and who knows the power of a great ebook, appearance no further than the Bookish Babe/Bro - the introvert's last romance partner.

The Low-Maintenance Lover

Introverts can often be considered "The Low-Maintenance Lover" in terms of romance. While some may additionally furthermore view introverts as being needy or high-protection in relationships, they regularly have a deep experience of independence and self-sufficiency that can reason them to fairly easygoing and espresso-protection partners.

For introverts, a low-renovation approach to romance frequently manner valuing extraordinary time over quantity. They might not want constant hobby or validation from their partner, who decide on as an alternative to comprehend the moments they do spend together. This can contain quiet evenings at home, exploring shared interests or interests, or in reality playing every other's corporation in comfortable silence.

The splendor of introverts as romance partners lies in their appreciation for the little things. They do now not need grand gestures or flashy shows of love to revel in cherished and preferred - a smooth cup of tea or heartfelt be conscious can do the trick.

This low-upkeep technique to romance may be specially effective for introverts, because it permits them to keep their revel in of independence at the same time as but fostering a deep and sizable reference to their accomplice.

So, in case you're searching out a partner who appreciates the little matters and values emotional intensity over floor-degree pleasure, appearance no further than the introvert - the draw close of low-protection romance.

The Heartfelt Homebody

Introverts can regularly be considered "The Heartfelt Homebody" as regards to romance. While some also can view introverts as being withdrawn or remoted, they frequently have a deep sense of consolation and contentment of their very own space. This revel in of domestic and belonging have to motive them to relatively heartfelt and nurturing partners.

For introverts, the residence may be a sanctuary wherein they'll retreat from the goals of the outdoor international and be themselves. They may moreover take terrific pleasure in growing a heat and alluring environment for themselves and their accomplice, with comfortable furniture, significant decor, and a focal point on coziness and rest.

However, it's miles important to be aware that every character and dating is specific, and there may be no character-duration-suits-all approach to romance. Some introverts can also furthermore have terrific goals and options of their relationships, and it's far vital to talk brazenly and definitely with one's accomplice to make certain that every people sense loved and valued.

Overall, introverts may be alternatively heartfelt and nurturing partners at the same time as given the space and independence to be themselves. By developing a warmth and welcoming environment, presenting emotional manual and empathy, and prioritizing emotional intimacy over outdoor wishes, introverts can create deep and massive connections with their partners that may ultimate an entire existence.

Chapter 10: The Creative Introvert

Are you a modern introvert? Congratulations, you're like a unicorn! Except as opposed to a horn, you've got a pen, paintbrush, or camera on your hand.

As a progressive introvert, you have got the superb functionality to reveal your inner worldwide into lovely works of art work. You do no longer need loud music, incredible lights, or a crowd of people to get stimulated. In reality, you'll probably determine upon a snug nook, a heat cup of tea, and a few peace and quiet.

But allow's be real, now and again being a modern introvert can be a piece of a assignment. Like if you have to community with a hard and fast of extroverted artists at a gallery putting in. Or even as your buddies want to go out and celebration, however you definitely need to live in and artwork on your present day masterpiece.

But worry now not, fellow progressive introverts! You have a thriller weapon: your creativeness. You can create entire worlds on your mind, and produce them to life on paper, canvas, or show. And of direction, you do now not want to be the lifestyles of the birthday celebration when you may be the author of the birthday party to your artwork.

So preserve on being you, innovative introvert. Embrace your quirks, comply with your passions, and keep making magic. Just take into account to come back lower back up for air and speak to a actual guy or ladies every on occasion. You in no way understand, they may definitely inspire your next masterpiece.

The Introvert's Advantage: How Introverts Excel in Creative Fields

Hey there, extroverts! You understand what they may be announcing, the early hen gets the computer virus, but the introvert gets the Pulitzer Prize.

That's right; introverts have a mystery advantage with regards to progressive fields.

While extroverts are busy speaking up a typhoon, introverts are quietly staring at the area round them, processing information of their personal unique manner, and springing up with wonderful thoughts.

Sure, extroverts is probably capable of sell their thoughts higher, however introverts have the superior product. They're similar to the Steve Jobs of the current worldwide; quietly innovating at the same time as virtually everybody else is distracted through the flashy advertising and advertising.

And allow's no longer neglect approximately the electricity of solitude. Introverts do not want a group of people to brainstorm thoughts. They can do it all on their non-public, with only a pen and paper (or a laptop, for the tech-savvy introverts available).

So next time you note an introvert sitting by myself at a coffee save, do now not assume they may be lonely or bored. They're probably just deep in concept, plotting their subsequent masterpiece. And who is aware about, possibly someday they'll be accepting an Oscar or a Grammy or a Nobel Prize, all manner to their introverted gain.

The Power of Solitude: How Introverts Use Alone Time to Foster Creativity

Ah, solitude. The introvert's favored interest. We do not want a therapist; we clearly want a few by myself time with our mind (and probable a few Netflix).

But did you recognize that solitude is in reality the call of the sport element to innovative fulfillment? While extroverts are to be had looking to brainstorm in a crowded room, introverts are thriving of their solo missions.

We introverts have mastered the artwork of being on my own, and it shows in our art work. We can sit down down for hours, in fact engrossed in our artwork, music, or writing, with out a care within the international.

And even as we do emerge from our caves, we come bearing the give up result of our exertions. Beautiful, concept-frightening, and occasionally downright bizarre creations that depart our extroverted opposite numbers scratching their heads.

So, extroverts, the following time you spot an introvert sitting by myself in a park or staring out of a window, don't worry about us. We're not lonely; we're actually basking in the glory of our solitude, cooking up the subsequent huge element. And who is aware about, perhaps inside the destiny you may be asking us for our autograph.

Empathy and Observation: How Introverts' Sensitivity Helps Them Create Compelling Art

Introverts won't have the loudest voices in the room, however we do have the maximum touchy ears. And eyes. And noses. Basically, we are like superheroes with heightened senses (truely with out the capes).

Our ability to take a look at the arena round us with such precision and intensity is what makes us incredible artists. We can pick out out up on subtle nuances in human conduct, word the tiniest data in nature, or maybe find the faintest whiff of idea within the air.

And our empathy? Forget approximately it. We're like strolling, speaking emotion detectors. We can revel in the unhappiness in a unhappy track, the joy in a glad portray, and the angst in a teenage diary.

So, at the identical time as extroverts is probably busy chatting up a hurricane, we introverts are silently soaking up the area around us, the use of our superhuman powers to create the maximum compelling art.

And in case you ever want a shoulder to cry on or someone to speak in confidence to, actually come to us introverts. We'll pay attention with our complete beings, and perhaps even flip your tale right proper into a stunning paintings of paintings.

The Quiet Confidence: How Introverts Embrace Their Unique Voice and Vision

Let's face it; extroverts can be a chunk loud and overbearing sometimes. But us introverts? We have a considered one in every of a kind shape of self warranty. We do not want to shout to make our voices heard. We allow our art speak for itself.

We're similar to the silent ninjas of the innovative global, quietly and with a bit of luck pursuing our visions even as not having to are attempting to find validation from others. We understand that our particular views and voices are precious, despite the fact that they do now not continuously wholesome the mainstream mold.

We don't want a fan membership or a swarm of social media fans to feel good about ourselves. We discover our without a doubt worth inside the art work we create, inside the effect we make on others, and in the pride of facts that we're dwelling our lives on our personal phrases.

So, extroverts, do now not mistake our quiet self assurance for shyness or lack of confidence. We apprehend who we're and what we're approximately, and we do not want to shout it from the rooftops to prove it. We'll definitely preserve doing our trouble, developing our artwork, and provoking others alongside the way.

Navigating the Creative World as an Introvert: Coping Strategies and Tips for Success

Ah, the contemporary global. It's a wild, loud, and every now and then overwhelming location. But lighten up, fellow introverts, we have got our thriller coping strategies to continue to exist and thrive on this chaos.

First, we have the conventional "cover in the rest room" method. Need a ruin from the noise and chatter? Just sneak away to the restroom for a couple of minutes of peace and quiet. No one will also word you are prolonged long long past (with any luck).

Next, we have were given the "fake it 'til you're making it" technique. This one's all approximately appearing assured and outgoing, even in case you're shaking to your boots at the inner. Just hold in mind to smile, nod, and possibly throw in some "it's far brilliant!"s or "splendid!"s for real diploma.

And if all else fails, there may be usually the "I'm a tortured artist" excuse. Need to cancel plans or bypass a celebration? Just tell people you're too busy developing masterpieces to socialize. They'll each count on you are a genius or a weirdo, but every manner, you'll have the notable excuse for fending off small communicate.

So, introverts, do no longer allow the loud and extroverted innovative worldwide get you down. Use those suggestions to navigate your way to success, one quiet step at a time.

Collaboration vs. Individual Creativity

Collaboration or going for walks solo? That is the eternal query for us introverts. On the best hand, we adore the liberty and manage of doing our very personal element. On the alternative hand, the idea of truly having to interact with one of a kind humans can deliver us proper into a panic.

But of course, there may be a middle floor. We can collaborate with others with out sacrificing our precious on my own time. It's referred to as the "digital collaboration" method. Basically, we honestly ship some emails back and forth, maybe a video name or two, and voila! We have efficiently collaborated at the identical time as no longer having to go away our relaxed little hideouts.

And if you do determine to task out into the real global for a collaborative mission, honestly undergo in thoughts to deliver snacks. Lots and hundreds of snacks. It's high-quality how lots less complicated it is to have interaction with human beings while there is meals worried.

In all seriousness, notwithstanding the truth that, collaboration may be a awesome manner for introverts to hold new perspectives and mind to their paintings. Just ensure to set barriers and take breaks whilst wanted, and you will be a collaborative movie star right away.

Chapter 11: The Introvert's Guide To Networking

My former boss stated that it's unusual that an introvert like me is aware of a way to work a room. By the give up of an occasion, I commonly have the industrial organization card of every new face, from team of workers to CEO. It's probably the most eldritch, however fondest praise I ever have been given at paintings.

Networking is a assignment, of course, but it doesn't propose it may't be a laugh!

1.   Networking for introverts is like going to a celebration in which you most effective realise the host's cat. But don't worry, that cat is a first rate verbal exchange starter!

2.   It's like being a spy, but in place of gathering intel, you are amassing commercial organization playing playing cards and elevator pitches.

three.   It's like being a ninja, but in preference to throwing stars, you're throwing your cautiously crafted private emblem.

four.   It's like playing a sport of chess, but in place of knights and bishops, you are strategizing your manner thru small speak and elevator pitches.

5.   Networking for introverts is like attempting to find to combination in at a celebration while you're sporting an entire-on Halloween gown. But whats up, now and again it's miles much less hard to be your self even as you're in disguise!

Remember, networking may no longer have to be a dreaded experience for introverts. Embrace your strengths, be yourself, and approach networking in a manner that feels real and snug to you. Who is privy to, you may simply make a few excellent connections or even enjoy the technique along the manner.

The Introvert's Fear of Networking Events

Here are a few funny takes at the introvert's worry of networking sports:

1. The excellent trouble scarier for introverts than a networking occasion is a wonder birthday celebration wherein they need to deliver a speech.

2. It's like being thrown into a lion's den, however in place of lions, there are extroverts armed with business agency cards and handshakes.

three. It's like being on a primary date, but in preference to finding love, you're attempting to find customers.

four. It's like being in a horror film, however in location of a killer with a chainsaw, it's the worry of awkward silences and now not knowledge what to mention.

5. For introverts, networking sports activities are like a skip among a dentist appointment and a hobby interview. Enough said.

Remember, it's right enough to experience annoying approximately networking activities as an introvert. But do now not permit fear preserve you lower lower back from making valuable connections and advancing your career. Embrace your strengths and technique networking in a manner that feels cushty and actual to you. And who's aware of, perhaps you could clearly have a few a laugh alongside the manner.

Strategies For Networking

Here are a few takes for networking:

1. Setting desires for networking is like setting dreams for a avenue journey. You want to understand in that you are going and how you will get there, but you also want to experience the adventure along the manner.

2. Practicing your elevator pitch is like training your pickup strains. You need to encounter as confident, charming, and remarkable, however with out sounding tacky or decided.

three. Following up with contacts is like following up with a crush. You do not want to be too pushy or clingy, but you moreover mght don't want to allow a wonderful opportunity slip away.

four. Networking is kind of a activity of chess. You want to be strategic, count on your opponent's actions, and be prepared to conform to converting times.

five. It's like going to a buffet, however rather than food, you're filling up your contacts listing with masses of interesting and treasured humans.

6. It's like taking region a diet, but in place of reducing out carbs, you are decreasing out small speak.

7. Networking like an introvert is like relationship in your 30s. You're no longer inquisitive about playing the sector anymore, you without a doubt want to find out a person who is actually well really worth a while and power.

eight. It's like being a ninja. You need to make strategic and centered moves to assemble relationships, without drawing too much interest to your self.

nine. Networking like an introvert is like gambling the extended pastime. You're inclined to position in the try and assemble right connections, even though it takes a bit longer to appearance effects.

10. It's like being a treasure hunter. You're not interested in collecting every piece of gold and silver, you clearly want to locate the gem stones which might be truly treasured and actually well worth a while.

Remember, networking does no longer need to be a numbers pastime. As an introvert, attention on constructing pleasant connections with people who percent your values and pursuits. And who's aware of, you would possibly simply discover some hidden treasures along the manner!

Chapter 12: The Benefits Of Being An Introvert

If you've reached this part of the e-book, then you definitely absolutely understand there are benefits to being an introvert. Here are a number of them, collectively with the ones referred to in extra detail in specific chapters:

1. Deep thinking and reflected photograph: Introverts are frequently tremendous thinkers who enjoy deliberating complicated troubles and thoughts. This ability to count on deeply and replicate on their studies can result in new insights and creative answers.

2. Strong listening skills: As introverts have a tendency to pay interest greater than they speak, they make bigger sturdy listening abilities. This allows them to choose up on essential records and nuances in conversations that others can also pass over.

3. Independence and self-sufficiency: Introverts are frequently cushty with solitude and self-reflected photo, that may cause more independence and self-sufficiency. They

are an lousy lot plenty less probably to depend on others for validation and are regularly capable of entertain themselves.

four. Empathy and statistics: Because introverts have a tendency to be precise listeners and thoughtful observers, they regularly have a more ability for empathy and information. They are capable of positioned themselves in other humans's footwear and spot topics from a couple of views.

5. Creativity and innovation: Introverts regularly have rich inner lives and can draw perception from their mind and studies. This can bring about particular and current ideas of their work and personal lives.

By recognizing and embracing the ones blessings, introverts can capitalize on their strengths and stay extraordinary lives that align with their personalities and values.

The Unique Strengths of an Introvert

Here are a few factors at the proper strengths that introverts bring to the desk:

1. Creativity: Introverts are first rate at wondering out of doors the sector, due to the fact let's face it, they spend a number of time of their very very personal packing containers.

2. Problem-solving: When confronted with a trouble, introverts are like detectives, constantly reading and thinking thru each detail. Just do no longer motive them to remedy the trouble in a crowded room.

3. Deep cognizance: When introverts popularity, they absolutely interest. It's like they have got a superpower that lets in them to tune out the whole global and hone in on what's crucial. Just make certain to offer them a heads up earlier than searching for to get their hobby.

4. Attention to element: Introverts are often detail-oriented and enjoy taking the time to make sure that matters are finished successfully. They have a tendency to interest at the small info that others can also overlook, which can be a valuable asset in masses of fields.

5. Empathy and facts: Introverts are often superb at listening and looking at, which allows them to understand others on a deeper diploma. They are able to positioned themselves in other humans's shoes and notice topics from a couple of views, which may be beneficial in plenty of conditions.

6. Observant: Introverts have a knack for noticing the little info that others may additionally moreover miss. It's like having a walking Sherlock Holmes for your crew.

7. Independent: Introverts are terrific at walking independently, because of the truth permit's be actual, once in a while special humans are only a distraction. Just do not be amazed if they arrive up with a genius concept after hours of solitary confinement.

By recognizing and leveraging these specific strengths, introverts need to make a valuable contribution in pretty some fields and industries. They deliver a completely precise mind-set and capability set that may be valuable in hassle-solving, creativity, and recognition.

How to Embrace Your Introversion and Use it to Your Advantage

Here are some strategies to embody your introversion:

1. Embrace your inner hermit: Instead of feeling accountable about staying in on a Friday night time time, encompass your internal hermit and enjoy the pride of an great e-book or film marathon.

2. Use your introverted superpowers: Introverts have the power of deep popularity and hobby to element - so use the ones powers for top, like crushing a bit mission or making plans the proper excursion.

3. Networking schmetworking: Who wants to community if you have a cosy blanket and a cup of tea? Embrace your introverted nature and pass the awkward, crowded networking sports in favor of constructing extensive connections with a pick few.

four. Enjoy the peace and quiet: Introverts want by myself time to recharge, so don't sense responsible about taking a ruin from socializing. Enjoy the peace and quiet, and are available decrease decrease back stronger and greater energized.

5. Lean into your quirks: Introverts regularly have precise pursuits and quirks, so consist of them! Whether it's miles a love of board video video video games or a fascination with nineteenth-century literature, lean into what makes you unique and have a good time it.

Remember, introversion is strength, not a susceptible aspect. Embrace your introverted nature and apply it to your advantage - you may truly surprise yourself with what you could accomplish!

Chapter 13: The Introvert's Guide To Self-Care

Self-care is crucial and additional so for introverts. Sometimes, the handiest subjects can convey the most delight. For instance, taking a long, warm bathe can be like a spa day within the consolation of your home. Or, curling up with a comfy blanket and watching your favourite film may be like a mini-excursion from the stresses of the arena.

Here are some takes on self-deal with introverts.

Self-take care of introverts is like charging your mobile smartphone - you want to take time to recharge your personal batteries, or you may run out of energy and crash.

It's like having a spa day, but as an alternative of having a massage, you are really taking a quiet bubble bath and analyzing a e-book.

It's like being your very personal private superhero, however instead of saving the sector, you are certainly saving your sanity thru the usage of taking some by myself time.

Self-cope with introverts is like being a cat - you want to take naps, stretch, and play with some toys to experience your fantastic.

It's like being a plant - you want a few by myself time to take within the solar and expand, however you furthermore may additionally want some water and vitamins (like pizza and Netflix) to thrive.

Self-care for introverts is kind of a spa day on your soul - however in desire to cucumber slices on your eyes, you have got got got a ebook for your hand and a "do no longer disturb" sign up your door.

Finding the proper by myself time interest is like finding the right pair of sweatpants - they may now not be fancy, but they're comfortable, relaxed, and make you sense you can address the area.

Remember, self-care is essential for everyone, introverts blanketed. So make an effort to lighten up and recharge, and do now not experience responsible approximately it!

Understanding the Importance of Self-Care for Introverts

As an introvert, neglecting self-care is like letting your mobile phone battery die inside the center of a road experience. You is probably capable of get thru manner of for a hint even as, but ultimately, the whole thing will come crashing down and you may be left feeling worn-out and overwhelmed.

Self-care is sort of a warmth blanket on a chilly winter night time time - it's far relaxed, comforting, and makes everything higher. As an introvert, taking time for yourself to recharge your batteries is vital to avoid burnout and hold your sanity.

Think of self-care as your introvert superpower - it's miles what offers you the power and resilience to face the world with self perception and beauty. So don't forget it, encompass it and allow it guide you toward a extra suit, happier lifestyles.

Identifying Your Personal Needs and Preferences

As an introvert, identifying your private dreams and alternatives is like in search of to treatment a Rubik's dice at the identical time as blindfolded. It's a daunting venture, but when you decide it out, you may sense like a genius.

Identifying yourself-care dreams is like choosing out your favourite taste of ice cream - it's miles all approximately private taste. Some introverts would possibly determine on curling up with an outstanding ebook, on the identical time as others may additionally decide on a chilled tub or an prolonged hike inside the outstanding exterior.

It's critical to realise what works for you, and what does now not. For instance, if you hate small talk and crowds, then attending a networking event might not be the satisfactory form of self-cope with you. Instead, you will probably discover greater solace in a quiet yoga beauty or a solo movie night time time.

So do no longer be afraid to check and try new topics. You never understand, you'll probable just find out your new favourite way to recharge your introverted batteries.

Establishing Healthy Boundaries

Establishing healthy boundaries as an introvert is like building a fortress around your highbrow fitness. You need to guard it from the outdoor international and make sure that simplest immoderate exceptional vibes are allowed in.

Saying "no" is just like the introvert's mystery weapon - it's far like having a get-out-of-prison-loose card in Monopoly. You can use it to avoid over self-discipline and protect your treasured on my own time.

Creating a peaceful and exciting surroundings is like building your private introvert oasis. It's wherein you may go to escape the chaos of the area and locate inner peace. So skip in advance, moderate some candles, placed on some soothing music, and bask in the glory of your introvert usa.

Remember, obstacles are like a safety machine in your intellectual fitness. So do not be afraid to set them up and protect your inner introvert sanctuary the least bit fees.

Developing a Self-Care Routine

Developing a self-care ordinary as an introvert is like placing together a puzzle. You want to discover the right quantities that during shape collectively to create a cute photograph of relaxation and rejuvenation.

Creating a steady normal is like training for a marathon, besides in desire to walking; you're education your mind to relax. You won't get a medal for it, however you may without a doubt revel in like a champion.

Incorporating self-care into a busy time table is like gambling Tetris together with your calendar. You want to healthy everything in handiest proper to make sure there may be enough time as a way to recharge your batteries.

Remember, self-care is type of a plant - it desires to be nurtured and tended to on the way to increase. So water yourself with a few calming tea, deliver yourself a few sunshine with an exceptional ebook, and watch your self bloom proper right into a happier, extra wholesome introvert.

Seeking Support When Needed

As an introvert, in search of beneficial aid while favored is like asking for guidelines while using. It may enjoy awkward, however it's higher than getting out of location and finishing up in a ditch.

Sometimes, absolutely everyone want a bit help from our pals. It's like at the equal time as you can't acquire that pinnacle shelf at the grocery store - you need someone to offer you a lift. Except in this example, it's far more like needing a person to enhance your morale and offer you with a pep speak.

Asking for assistance is like admitting you're not satisfactory, that may be a hard pill to swallow for any introvert. But the truth is, no character's awesome, and searching out guide is a sign of power, now not weakness.

So do now not be afraid to attain out to a chum, family member, or perhaps a therapist even as you need it. They can be like a lifestyles raft in a sea of overwhelm and tension, supporting you live afloat and navigate the choppy waters of life.

Chapter 14: The Introvert's Path To Success

So how do you outline an introvert's route to achievement in maintaining off society's pressures and norms and being authentic to your self? Here are some takes.

Success for an introvert is like planting a seed. You need to nurture it, offer it time and area to increase, and on occasion sprinkle a few water (or espresso) on it. And if all else fails, just fake you alleged to plant a cactus. Plus, you get to position on a fancy hat at the identical time as you do it.

The introvert's direction to achievement is like trekking a mountain. It can be a chunk of a climb, but once you attain the top, you get to revel in the view and revel in like a total boss. Plus, you get to position on a fab backpack entire of snacks.

The introvert's adventure to fulfillment is like strolling a marathon. You need to tempo yourself, live targeted, and every now and then take a harm to stretch your legs (or binge-watch Netflix). And in case you really need to win, without a doubt fake the quit line is a snug mattress looking ahead to you on the cease.

Achieving achievement as an introvert is like completing a puzzle. You want to discover the proper quantities, healthy them collectively in the appropriate manner, and now and again take a step again to recognize your art work. Plus, you get to place on cushty pants and consume snacks even as you do it.

Success as an introvert is like getting a tan inside the color - it takes a piece more attempt, however it's far truely doable with the right technique.

It's like in search of to win a recreation of chess in competition to an extrovert - they may make flashy movements and talk a massive recreation, however that slow and steady wins the race.

It's like trying to bake the right soufflé - you want to carefully study the recipe, have staying strength, and keep away from any surprising movements or loud noises.

Success as an introvert is like reading a complicated board interest - it takes time to research the pointers and method, but when you do, you could dominate the sport (and initiate your friends).

Remember, introverts can acquire remarkable success through gambling to their strengths and finding a route that works for them. And do not forget to have a hint fun alongside the way!

Success Stories of Famous Introverts

Let's test a few introverted icons who have made it big. While some have by no means explicitly declared themselves as introverts, they showcase some of the not unusual traits. Plus, they are all immensely a fulfillment and taken into consideration as inspirations and models on what is feasible:

1. Bill Gates: The brains behind Microsoft is concept for his introverted nature. He loves

to spend his time considering the destiny of era and diving deep into his mind.

2. J.K. Rowling: Despite her social anxiety, Rowling's imagination soared and made her one of the most a hit authors ever.

three. Albert Einstein: The well-known scientist changed into infamous for his introversion, frequently spending time out of place in idea instead of socializing. Yet, his contributions to physics revolutionized the world.

four. Warren Buffett: The CEO of Berkshire Hathaway keeps a low profile and shies some distance from public interest.

5. Mark Zuckerberg: The founder of Facebook can be one of the most successful tech entrepreneurs of his technology, however he is also stated for being pretty non-public and rarely giving interviews or public appearances.

6. Barack Obama: The former President is an introvert who prefers spending time on my

own or with a small enterprise of near pals. Despite this, he gave powerful speeches and related with large audiences in the end of his presidency.

7. Emma Watson: The actress and activist is candid about the worrying conditions she faced dealing with sudden reputation and interest after starring within the Harry Potter films, however her introverted individual helped her find out a way to control.

eight. Steven Spielberg: The famous director is understood for spending plenty of time on my own, walking on his movies and mind. Despite his introverted nature, he has created a number of the maximum a hit and awesome movies in records.

These introverted icons display us that being introverted may be an asset in area of a impediment. With the right mind-set and approach, introverts can gather brilliant achievement in their fields.

Chapter 15: Overcoming Introvert Stereotypes

Here are a few stereotypes of introverts. I'm effective you've heard at least one in each of them:

Introverts are often seen as being aloof or snobbish, however in truth we are definitely in our private little worlds. It's like we are dwelling in a Harry Potter invisibility cloak that quality works on social situations.

People assume introverts do not need to party, but we truly birthday party in our personal way. We're much more likely to have a Netflix and sit back night time than a loopy night time time out, however we nevertheless apprehend the way to have a exquisite time.

Some human beings count on introverts are inclined or shy, but we are certainly definitely more selective about wherein we placed our electricity. It's like we are strategic ninjas, carefully choosing our battles and keeping our electricity for at the same time as we really want it.

The stereotype is that introverts are lousy at socializing, but clearly we really have our very own fashion. It's like we're gambling a one-of-a-kind activity of chess, in which we carefully plan our actions and strategize our conversations.

People expect introverts are anti-social, but we in reality determine upon to socialize in smaller, extra intimate settings. It's like we're the penguins of the social global, cozying up with a few near buddies in region of flocking collectively in massive crowds.

Remember, introverts are not one-dimensional beings. We have loads of strengths, interests, and strategies of socializing. Don't be afraid to mission the stereotypes and embody your precise introverted self!

The Introvert's Battle Against Stereotypes

Introvert stereotypes - because of the reality seemingly, we're all imagined to be shy, silly wallflowers who in no way want to head away our houses. As if!

Yet my fellow introverts - we are able to fight lower decrease lower back within the path of those stereotypes with a bit humor. Here are some funny takes at the introvert's war in opposition to stereotypes:

"I'm no longer shy, I'm really searching forward to someone to provide you with a higher communique starter than 'So, what do you do?'"

"I'm now not antisocial, I truly select out to socialise by myself terms. Like, you recognize, as soon as I enjoy discover it irresistible."

"I'm not unfriendly, I just have a resting 'depart me on my own' face."

"Just due to the truth I do now not enjoy small talk does no longer imply I'm now not a fun and thrilling man or woman. I suggest, have you ever ever ever heard me cross on a rant about my favourite e-book?"

"I won't be the life of the birthday celebration, however I'm the handiest you need to be friends with at the same time as you want a person to binge-watch a whole season of a TV display with."

Being an introvert does now not recommend I'm shy or antisocial. It certainly manner I honestly have a wholesome respect for my on my own time, like a cat taking a sleep.

People suppose introverts are unfriendly, however in reality we are simply maintaining our power for at the same time as we need to be amazing. It's like a battery saver mode on a mobile phone.

Just due to the truth I do no longer like small talk does not suggest I'm awful at networking. I can although make sizeable connections, like a ninja blending into the shadows.

Yes, I'm quiet, but that doesn't advise I'm no longer assured in who I am. I'm like a stealthy superhero, silently kicking stereotypes to the decrease.

Introverts are not simply bookworms and wallflowers. We have precise strengths that we supply to the desk, like a mystery weapon prepared to be unleashed.

Remember, introvert stereotypes are just that - stereotypes. Don't allow them to outline you and do no longer be afraid to expose off your particular and high-quality introverted characteristics!

How to Educate Others About Introversion

Here's a address the manner to train others approximately introversion:

Hold a seminar titled "Introversion: It's no longer most effective for vampires and moody young adults."

Make a PowerPoint presentation providing graphs and charts evaluating the advantages of by myself time in location of socializing. Bonus elements for which include lovely cat films.

Carry spherical a laminated card with bullet points of introvert information to whip out on every occasion someone questions your social behavior.

Offer to change places with an extrovert for a day and spot who comes out more exhausted through the cease of it.

Hand out "I'm an Introvert" buttons and project people to wear them for a day to raise awareness for introversion. Bonus elements for designing an same "I'm an Extrovert" button to reveal team spirit.

Remember, education others about introversion may want to now not should be critical commercial organisation. Have amusing with it and show off your unique humorousness!

Chapter 16: The Future Of Introversion

Here are some takes on the Future of introversion:

The destiny of introversion is asking super - so long as we are able to preserve to have digital meetings and make money working from home in our sweatpants.

With the upward push of social media, introverts ultimately have a way to talk without having to actually communicate to human beings. The future's searching awesome!

The future of introversion is all approximately developing relaxed, introvert-outstanding areas where we are able to recharge our batteries and keep away from any useless small communicate.

As generation continues to enhance, we will speedy have AI assistants that could control all of our social interactions for us. Finally, introverts may additionally additionally have a private assistant that virtually is conscious them!

The destiny of introversion is all approximately embracing our particular strengths and the use of them to make the arena a better vicinity. So, basically, introverts will ultimately take over the arena - but quietly and from the consolation of our private homes.

Remember, the destiny of introversion is what we make it. So allow's encompass our strengths, challenge stereotypes, and preserve to thrive in a worldwide that won't constantly understand us.

The Introvert's Bright Future

Here are a few humorous takes on the future of introversion:

The destiny is calling bright for introverts - we might ultimately get our personal island wherein we are capable of truly take a seat once more and take a look at books in peace.

I listen introverts will brief be able to get a diploma in "Netflix and Chill" - sooner or later, a profession course that speaks to us!

With more humans embracing introversion, I wager we are going to see some wild new inventions - like noise-canceling headphones in your complete house.

I can't watch for the day while introverts are the brand new cool children at the block - forget about partying until sunrise, we will be those who every body desires to invite over for a enterprise night time time.

I expect that introverts will fast take over the arena - quietly, of direction, however with a fierce dedication at the manner to surprise each person.

Predictions On Wow Introversion Will Shape the World

Well, allow me dust off my crystal ball and see what I can come up with for this one:

We might also see an increase in virtual truth socializing, permitting introverts to engage with others without leaving the consolation in their houses. Finally, we are able to attend events in our pajamas without all and sundry knowing!

With the upward thrust of far off art work, we'd see a decline in conventional workplace regions and a more emphasis on developing cushty, introvert-pleasant artwork environments. Think: plush couches, clean lights, and loads of snacks.

As self-care will become extra mainstream, we might see an influx of introvert-centered nicely being retreats. Imagine a spa day wherein you may have a examine your selected e-book in peace on the identical time as sipping on tea, with out everyone interrupting you.

And in the end, with introverts taking up management roles in numerous industries, we would see a shift inside the direction of extra considerate, introspective selection-making techniques. Just do not expect us to make those options for the duration of a noisy, crowded assembly.

How to Stay True to Your Introverted Nature

How do you live true for your introverted nature on the same time as adapting to the converting global round you?

Just due to the fact some distance off paintings is turning into extra common does not propose you want to surrender your property workplace, AKA your couch.

If the arena becomes extra introvert-exceptional, possibly we are going to in the end get a few peace and quiet in consuming places and film theaters.

As mental fitness will become a bigger popularity, introverts can in the long run say, "I informed you so" to all of the ones extroverts who claimed we had to exit and socialize greater.

With the upward thrust of online communique, we introverts can ultimately display off our expert typing skills and witty textual content banter.

As self-care will become extra famous, we're capable of proudly tell human beings that we had been taking bubble baths and reading books lengthy in advance than it have become modern-day-day. We had been actually beforehand of the curve!

Chapter 17: Understanding Your Introvert Nature

Quick question: Are you high-quality partying 24/7, 3 hundred and sixty 5 days a year, with clearly sufficient hours to sleep and relaxation? Or are you amazing operating and resting for your room all of the days of the 12 months and excellent going out for groceries?

The fact is that it is no longer possibly each person goes to nod to any of those questions – at least not the not unusual man or woman. Unless you've got got got taken vows to live in a cave praying for this sinning worldwide, or some bolts and nuts upstairs have turn out to be a bit worn out, you are not going to live both like a hermit or stay wild like it is all adrenaline and now not anything else for your frame. In short, you and every incredible man or woman need some time out for amusement and a while on my own. The query is – in what percentage? It is from that balanced perspective that you could then fairly say that you are an extrovert whilst you want to be out with people extra than you need to be alone. And the other is the case for an introvert.

Now, if we confine you to an administrative center to art work for us all day prolonged and make you've got were given your lunch indoors; and first-class release you to transport domestic within the night, does that make you an introvert? You had been by myself maximum of the day, haven't you? And if we supply you to the fields to work in a difficult and rapid and only allow you to be on my own even as going to sign in your day's salary, does that make you an extrovert? The solution isn't always any. Reason...? You see – the idea of being each introverted or extroverted is not a desire. It is inherent. It is biological. You neither have a desire in it nor does your boss or absolutely everyone else for that rely. How so, you could wonder?

The Making of an Introvert and an Extrovert

You see, I can not end which you are an introvert really due to the truth I actually have decided you by myself; much like I can not deduce you are an extrovert just because I noticed you in a party. The difference among an introvert and an extrovert is essentially the surroundings that makes each of them energized.

What energizes an extrovert is being round people at the same time as for an introvert, it's miles being by myself. You see, each a part of your body has an important feature to play – properly, perhaps except the appendix; that piece of muscle this is lots hassle while infected and desires no replacement as soon as eliminated. With the cerebral cortex, it desires to be aroused to a certain diploma so that you can sense thoroughly. And really, the level of arousal is pretty high already for introverts. The component right here is that there are humans whose cerebral cortex is already biologically inspired; and so being in a place that is distinctly charged with many people bothers them – they could get confused and uncomfortable and begin to lose their valuable power. Such humans choose to be by myself longer — the introverts.

Conversely, there are those people whose cerebral cortex isn't always biologically optimally inspired. As such, they want to be amongst humans to get better charged. Whenever such humans are on my own for extended periods, they commonly usually generally tend to come to be uncomfortable or maybe unsettled and as a end result lose electricity unnecessarily. For that motive, they favor to be among humans and in a place with hundreds of hobby — the extroverts.

Now, because of the fact people are biologically stimulated at extraordinary ranges you can't then lump absolutely everyone together as being completely introverted or genuinely extroverted. People have a piece of this and a bit of that. Of direction a few humans will lean extra within the route of introversion at the same time as others will lean towards the opposite direction. This clarification comes out thoroughly from the research of the '60s made via Psychologist Hans Eysenck.

And so you realise it isn't always pretty much humans in keeping with se however approximately the detail of stimulation, check those people whom you're announcing are introverted and others you discover as being extroverted. Whenever rewards are being dished out, even when in non-public, that pride of your extrovert is seen even as an introvert will usually hold a groovy disposition. In short, rewards are stimulating to an extrovert. Understand it this way, if you may – that the introvert already has a extremely good diploma of dopamine in the cerebral cortex and goals no more; or little greater counting on each character. And the alternative is the case with an extrovert. And it is ideal that you admire dopamine as that chemical responsible for your motivation.

Chapter 18: The Power Of Introverts

Have you seen a land snail? Well, this one travels with its shell. It genuinely remains internal that shell until it chooses to expose itself. Now that is the analogy you could supply to an introvert because of the truth regardless of how chaotic the sector becomes, the introvert can determine to brush aside you all and the whole lot spherical and clearly be alongside with his or her internal self. That is a bonus over an extrovert who can't pressure people to come out and offer enterprise and pleasure. In quick, an introvert can retract to the maximum appropriate environment for her or him nearly at will.

And because being introverted isn't tantamount to being always shy, an introvert can accomplish as lots as an extrovert can. Unfortunately, many humans do now not understand that and they maintain overlooking the talents of the introvert. It is time we cited that there is a lot of proper that we leave out out only for not giving possibilities to introverts. Of direction you are not going to have a look at in shape to your enterprise employer after acquiring the important statistics concerning introverts. Just think about the most impacting introverts the sector has had over the years – collectively with Mahatma Gandhi; Rosa Parks; Eleanor Roosevelt; and others.

In fact, the studies artwork of Psychologists Gregory Feist in league with Mihaly Csikszentmihalyi elements out that the maximum modern lot in maximum fields occur to be introverts. And you, manifestly, recognise that it is in being modern that you get matters finished. And it is in getting subjects done which you get your profession growing; your corporation thriving and increasing; and masses more enhancing. According to creator Susan Cain, introverts have extremely good developments, which embody:

Taking time to count on before speaking

Avoiding battle

Being capable of pay hobby with relative ease

Not getting effects bored

Let us notably have a look at how you may tell which you lean more towards being introverted than in the direction of being extroverted:

You have a tendency to think the tons much less you're the better

This mentality is not due to the fact you're advocate in provisions or something like that; it is genuinely which you typically generally tend to get beaten thru being amongst many people. When it includes interacting you make a decision upon a one on one communication in choice to random chit chat. And do you understand how heaps powerful a custom designed dialogue is compared to mere chit chat?

You find it powerful to be on my own

This is the time to check your past wellknown normal overall performance in an purpose way. It is likewise the time to relax and rejuvenate. On the general, it is this by myself time that you even beautify your universal overall overall performance. But does the place realise this? Everyone appears to say you are doing now not whatever at the same time as you're successfully enjoyable and doing what's definitely vital for super usual overall performance.

Feeling like your head is ready to explode

You get this sense whilst you're an introvert because of the reality your mind is typically busy even when you are by myself. Brain scans have already proven that during medical research. And in order that feeling that leads you to seeking out a few quiet location is affirmation that you are this kind of human beings whose thoughts is probably on an overdrive even when humans see you absolutely quiet and reputedly blank.

Being tempted to make pointless experience visits to the toilet

You understand the way you're tempted to close your place of work door and take a catnap if you have been up all night time for some reason and rarely have been given to sleep? That is the identical way you sense approximately dashing to the relaxation room, albeit for 5min and and now not the use of a bladder issues, while your thoughts feels crushed.

Having the urge to go away a party as quick as you get there

This feeling that a minute or so of partying is all you want is generally a sign of being an introvert. And there is not whatever incorrect with the sensation; or maybe the real leaving.

Finding the cellular phone especially intrusive

It is a sign of being introverted no longer wishing to be on cell cellphone regularly and for eternity. And generally you could dislike the reality that the ringing of the phone is interrupting your concept way. Try and keep in mind we indicated that an introvert's thoughts is already inspired and lively even without outdoor affect.

Preferring few meaningful friendships to many informal friendships

It is herbal for introverts to discover their lives wealthy with simplest a handful of pals of their pretty calm global. And in those styles of conditions, you realize that such few friendships are more intimate and precious. That does now not endorse that an introvert does no longer have associates – no; but the introvert does now not mistake the ones for something else. This is certainly the same of the choice for one on one talk with one or two people in location of chit chat with one 0 one humans.

Dreading being concerned in aim market participation

If you experience like hiding below the seat at the same time as an actor is seeking out reaction from people in the target marketplace, it's miles in fact, a signal of being introverted. It is just as lousy whilst someone is pulling out to the dance floor. Yet you occasionally enjoy dancing.

So, are you capable of do what extroverts do at the identical time as you're an introvert?

Yes, you may. However, the concept is doing what extroverts do on your very personal phrases. It is like – your thoughts isn't always over-engaged; you do not experience over-stimulated; so, at the time, you can do with some out of doors stimuli. In brief, when you have to do the ones subjects that extroverts do, it desires to be at your very very own time and to your preferred degree. That is the only way you will be comfortable with it.

Then again, in order to ensure you are cushty with the entire enterprise, because you are not used to it except – like speaking in advance than an target market – you perform a little unique degree of practice. And this form of education, you do within your non-public consolation location.

Chapter 19: Making Friends As An Introvert

You have already registered the misconception many people have approximately introverts; that they do not kind of like people or even to be in happy locations. What you need is if you want to manual distinct introverts into getting the sort of pals as a manner to not motive them to stress or stressful situations. In fact, in advance on we stated some thing to do with introverts doing what extroverts do but on their character phrases.

Whereas you're able to essential and being social those factors will help:

It is certainly useful to watch out for social burnout

What this basically way is that while you socialize along with your pals and all your extrovert colleagues, you need now not attempt to hold up with actually everyone else. Trying to preserve up with the Joneses has in no way helped every body – you simply grow to be dry, harassed and depressing. Here, you may emerge as low on energy; burdened; and, of route, depressing.

So, stay on the social location as long as you revel in top notch. Beyond that truly zoom into your cocoon – it does you correct and also you understand it. If it method wearing yourself bodily out of the area, truly pass ahead. In quick, you have got were given were given controlled to make friends for the period you had your excessive; and you could connect to them at a later time.

You want as a way to pick out out your buddies as it should be

The point proper right here is that during place of being the character to move for social gatherings to which you are invited, why no longer be one to put together activities and invite humans? You are not horrible in control tendencies just because of the reality you are an introvert. And while you are calling the pix you have got the leeway to ask those who are greater or an lousy lot a good deal less together with you – introverts. These are those who will now not exhaust you with express show of excitement and relentless talk.

In fact, in this era of technology, you may preserve in contact on the facet of your preference of buddies through SMS; WhatsApp; Twitter; and all options of social media. You can even have scheduled gatherings together collectively with your form of pals; your venue and timing being your choice. So as you may see, you are making friends for your terms and you could truly have your social circle grade by grade expand without a person of you feeling crushed.

You Do Not Have To Copy the Extrovert

What does that propose? Well, it manner which you do no longer have go out without a harm; strive to speak to each person in the room; try to be audible above anyone else; and also you do now not even want to draw the attention of various people. Rather:

1. Reach out to few people and deliver them interest

You are one for quality and you are aware about it. So if you try and unfold your self too thin you may turn out to be feeling disillusioned, and in this example of socializing, even exhausted. Yet with the few people that you meet, you may look at more about them and in the technique even enjoy cushty to speak in self assurance to them. That is a certain way of making pleasant friendship this is sustainable and robust.

2. Talk about the trouble at hand and others that arise – not you

Just because of the truth extroverts will be inclined to attract hobby onto themselves isn't always any reason why you need to try and do the same. It is higher that you try and are looking for facts from the opportunity people so you get to examine what they suppose and what they pick out. It is a extraordinary manner of creating human beings together with you for taking interest in them. Let them apprehend that you are open to them. That manner, they will apprehend that regardless of the reality that they do now not get to appearance numerous you later it isn't because of the reality you do no longer like them. And you may find out such humans going out of their manner to ask you in destiny after they have a few thing they would love to percent with you.

three. Give an opinion

If there can be room to participate with out speaking about your self, via all technique, permit the rest understand your opinion. You will clearly be letting it seemed that being an introvert isn't equal to being daft. After all, there are numerous introverts whose names are not approximately to move away humans's minds speedy and that virtually due to their wise contributions to the world – people like Albert Einstein and Bill Gates.

4. Regulate your outings

Why ought to you want to go out together with your extrovert buddies who are searching for a exceptional deal desired stimulation, and then you definately begin to enjoy overwhelmed and de-energized?

Those extrovert pals of yours will no longer despise you truely you make a decision to take a breather. In truth, if you display them that your style is that shape of regulated a laugh, they will get used to it.

five. Summon your staying electricity

Often extroverts need quick reactions which can be entire of satisfaction. But you are the deep philosopher; that man or woman who desires to ensure of what they will be announcing in advance than they mouth it. And you do no longer with out issues show excitement. So, those humans are possibly to skip directly to someone else and likely take lengthy before coming another time to you. Keep your cool – it isn't their fault. Once they get to learn how resourceful you may be, they may constantly slot you in somewhere a few thing it takes. And they may charge your friendship too.

Chapter 20: Surviving A World That Never Stops Talking

The international is chatty; the arena has loads of movements; and the arena is typically one chaotic scene. The question is: do you have were given an opportunity whether or no longer or not to be an actor or no longer? Truth – no, you don't. Until they locate every different liveable planet, we are tied to our worrying earth. And so it's far up to you to make the splendid out of what there's.

Is it viable to alter the vicinity to in form the introvert? Let us honestly say if it changed into going to rain, it although shall. And if the solar was going to shine, it surely goes to shine. This isn't always a case of you transferring the mountain but a case of you finding the leeward factor of the mountain and a few difficulty specific location suits you pleasant. In short, you need to inform yourself which you are inherently an introvert and no man or woman offers a hoot about that. In any case, being an introvert is not a disadvantage. How many introverts enter a meeting room with out a idea what cause of motion needs to be taken and become producing the high-quality blueprint for the undertaking? They be aware of loaded factors from extroverts eager to be heard after which they weigh the ones in competition to countering mind from in addition extroverted participants; and that they become with a smooth write-up.

Still, you may satisfactory pay attention to this a whole lot before you begin to become irritable and confused. So have some strategies of survival.

1) Having an escape plan

Are we announcing you sneak out? Well, in case you are in a meeting it isn't a realistic idea to certainly steal your manner out. But there is always the rest room, bear in mind? Those 5min, which you may exchange into 10min to serve your reason, are very available in stabilizing your feelings.

But in case you are speakme of a party, simply make certain you are not tied to someone that you haven't any have an impact on over. Like in case you are tied to the identical technique of transport with a few extrovert who could need to stay at the birthday party till morning, you'll be in hassle. You had higher exit through cab and ensure you have enough cash for a cab lower back domestic. That manner you may be loose to move away the birthday party after making one preferred spherical to ensure as many human beings as possible take a look at for your presence.

2) Develop an attitude of starting up small communicate

Chirping might not be your vicinity of understanding – that, we get. But assume you took it upon your self to keep one or souls that discover activities as torturous as you do? You should say good day at random and try to make small speak. You see you will be hitting birds with the same stone – making friends similarly to rescuing an introvert which include you. And bet what? That can be the exquisite pass you ever made the whole day because of the fact proper there might also moreover additionally emerge actual friendships.

And did you realize small talk is what offers you common floor with nearly everybody? It can be the climate; the internet web page visitors; making a song skills; and such. As long as you maintain the whole lot desired at the onset, you will be right for conversation.

3   They is probably glad to interact with you

How do you recognize? That is the component. How do you apprehend that they wouldn't? When you're an introvert, you'll be predisposed to expect that humans are not inquisitive about your presence or what you keep in mind subjects. Yet that is your misguided belief coming from the fact that an awful lot attention appears to be going to the extroverts. And in case you recall it significantly, you do not even need half of that interest. Whenever it threatens to go back your manner you sense like burying your self below the desk or pray which you soften into nothingness.

So, attempt to introduce yourself to people no matter whether or not they may be introverts or extroverts. If they show no hobby, what's it to you? You understand you have got got lots to offer in phrases of thoughts just so they lose out on that. And via the manner, snobs are just snobs – they do not have to be extroverts.

4) Identify your redeeming spot

If that could be a region you return to regularly both for workplace talents or other social capabilities, understand a gap in which you can cross and hide from the corporation for some time. A huge resort is possibly to have some park in which you could take a walk or perhaps a few quiet front room in which you could take a seat like a equipped visitor.

And if it is on the administrative center, you may take your breaks in the Board Room. After all, the entire company is conscious at the same time as the bigwigs of the Board are round – so that you cannot be stuck unawares.

5) Build yourself a wealth of peace in advance

Whenever you are about to exit to a loud place, make sure you've got had been given had hundreds of time to yourself. That way you may be so cool that it's going to take a whole lot of chaos to destabilize.

6) Enter a place with pre-set desires

One detail as a manner to hold you from feeling like fish out of water is being busy at the side of your thoughts. And due to the truth you are used to concentrating, the notable way to discover a few element to concentrate on is having a few aspect set to do. Let us say you have been invited to an corporation of kinds. You may also want to determine properly earlier that taken into consideration one in every of your priorities can be to recognize the representatives of your community branch.

Now, for the cause that that isn't statistics you are going to discover on the menu, you will have to speak to someone and ask. Is asking speaking? Yes. Are you going to be rude and start asking topics without introducing your self? No. And proper right here you can see how smooth it is to make communication with out being self conscious and moreover on your non-public terms. And further, you get to understand one more person who became now not in your checklist – the handiest you're searching for information from. If you have got got three or 4 such objects for your time table, tell me if definitely you could have room to lose interest. At least you'll maintain your self the temptation to go away right away on arrival – due to the truth you can have a personal venture.

I desire with the aid of manner of the use of now you've got observed that you had been doing more of a one-on-one and not a crowd hassle. Again you have not left your mind wander idly. This scenario pretty locks out any chatter and noise going on around you because of the fact you handiest cope with what pursuits you. That is how you get to live to inform the story in a global that has talk coming from all commands of the compass.

www.ingramcontent.com/pod-product-compliance
Lightning Source LLC
Chambersburg PA
CBHW071443080526
44587CB00014B/1967